Morris from Beth & John

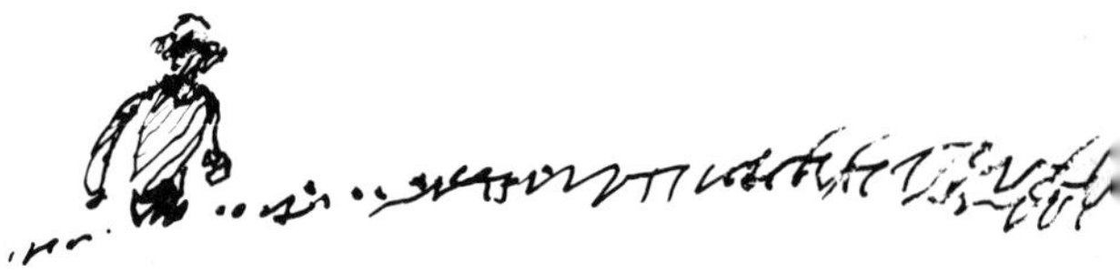

I Remember

GALLERY BOOKS An Imprint of W. H. Smith Publishers Inc.   112 Madison Avenue New York City 10016

AMERICA

Eric Sloane
1971

Produced by Claygill Books, Inc.
Published by
GALLERY BOOKS
An imprint of W.H. Smith Publishers Inc.
112 Madison Avenue, New York,
New York 10016

DESIGNED BY JUDITH WORACEK BARRY

MANUFACTURED IN ITALY
ISBN 0-8317-4971-7

OTHER BOOKS BY ERIC SLOANE

Table of Contents

This painting hangs in the lobby of the small museum in Kent, Connecticut, that houses my collection of early American tools. A hand scythe for cutting grain hangs from a nail in the massive beam brace, along with a leather-thonged flailing club for thrashing grain. The semi-circular wooden implement leaning against the barn door is a winnowing tray for scooping up the thrashed grain and tossing it in the wind so that the chaff blows away and the heavier whole grain falls back into the tray. The barn itself was torn down, but the door shown here was saved and is now the entrance to my studio in nearby Warren.

Author's reason for a book

REMEMBERING THE STORIES OF SARAH BERNHARDT'S numerous "farewell tours" and Buffalo Bill's endless "final appearances," I decided against starting this book by announcing it as my last, though that had been my first intention. Probably, without any attempt at being melodramatic, I wanted only to convince myself that I am old and tired enough to abandon the typewriter desk for a softer seat at my easel and to spend the rest of my time at pleasurable painting.

In these adventurous years of abstract expression, purposeful writing—like purposeful living—has nearly lost its appeal. But being old-school and hopelessly realistic, I cannot rid myself of the conviction that life and all its arts should exist for definite and good reasons. I feel called upon, therefore, to announce my purpose in compiling this book. Putting it together was nothing less than a labor of love (as all things we do in this life should be), because to me recollection is a special pleasure. Benjamin Franklin, another sentimental realist, said, "The next best thing to living one's life over again seems to be the recollection of that life, and to make that recollection as durable as possible by putting it all down in writing."

Most of my lifetime has been spent in painting and writing, with the steadfast purpose of either reviving or retrieving certain worthwhile things of the American past, yet always without being bitter about present-day devastation. Perhaps my nostalgic dreams did hide an occasional bitterness, but the richness and pleasure derived from rekindling earlier times overcame it. I think I simply left animosity and criticism to the angry young men of my time. But now, in good and patriotic cause, I ask the right to become an angry *old* man, because in my heart for a long while there has been a small voice of despair for the survival of America which I believe deserves to be heard at this time.

I trust you will find more hope than doubt in my book. Thoreau said, "Faith keeps many doubts in her pay. If I could not doubt, I should not believe." Yet Thoreau lived in a comparatively contented era, as reflected by the artists of his time. Most of the painters who portrayed the American scene as it was during that quiet age found little to quarrel with. Social comment by the artist was confined to caricaturing; fine art caused no arguments—it was peaceful conversation. But quarrel is now the first order of our day, and powerful as peaceful conversation

1

may be, it becomes weak and is often lost completely in the din of disorder and rebellion. I remember that de Gaulle, when writing his memoirs, took a phrase from Shakespeare and began with "To be great is to carry on a great quarrel." You will find very few quiet, rural landscapes portrayed in modern art, because such scenes encompass no quarrel for these artists to depict.

The performance of living has become a quarrel instead of an enjoyable experience. I remember American humor and when there were American humor magazines like the old *Life* and *Judge* and American professional cartoonists whose business it was to make people laugh. Then, of a sudden it seems, American humor spent itself and collapsed. Humor magazines failed and even "comic" strips became anything but comic, featuring cowboys and gangsters and detectives and supermen who rarely said anything funny, like Mutt and Jeff or Happy Hooligan or the Katzenjammers. A sense of humor has long been an American trait; true, it is illusion but it carried us through hard times. It could serve us well today, for as Mark Twain observed "the secret source of humor is not joy but sorrow; there is no humor in heaven."

The challenge for the survival of America is currently much greater than it was when our country began because now we are confused millions instead of a dedicated few. Moderation, peace, decency, freedom, discipline, devotion to country, reverence for God—almost everything on which our nation was originally founded, are suddenly on trial: the real danger is that we tolerate it. In the blind faith that their truth will save them, we accept and even encourage attacks on our national heritage; we accept it as a temporary tantrum and a cycle that will soon pass. We frequently lean backward to the point of losing balance, while components of our national heritage disappear one by one.

As far as our beautiful countryside is concerned, that particular part of the American heritage has already gone wherever we have "developed" it. The urge to become rich at the expense of the land, to commercialize the countryside at the expense of the landscape, is a recognized national trait. The winds of change certainly have reached tornadolike speed in devastating our landscape.

Already the very word "landscape" has lost its original meaning of "what God put there"; now it usually refers to "a view built by man." As we become richer in other things, the beauty of our natural American heritage becomes poorer at the staggering rate of as much as one hundred square miles each day. There are almost no landscapes left between most towns where business parallels the highway and spreads out to touch the next town's conglomerate of ugliness. You may travel countless miles from town to town without seeing any natural countryside at all—just one continuous roadside tapestry of bad taste.

It comes as a blow to me that even the most commonplace sights and sounds of a few decades ago are either going or have already gone. It might seem trivial to most people today that the tinkle of cowbells or the steady chant of axes and saws in the forest were once unforgettable country music; now they are gone, replaced by the buzz of power saws in the woods and by the sputter and cough of tractors.

The music of soft sounds and the comfort of quiet, trivial as they may now seem, were important in the vanished American life. I find that many of my guests from the city actually need noise to fall asleep: they are kept awake by the thunder of silence and the soft, tiny sounds typical of a country place.

The city person gets so accustomed to the litter of sound that he finally thrives on the diet of noise-polluted air.

Country lanes, tree-vaulted streets, spired churches, river ferries, and rural railroad stations, so recently a part of my everyday, are more examples of the American past. I am sad that tomorrow's youth will never know a simple harvest, see a haystack, hear a steam-locomotive whistle, sleep in a hay barn, or fish in a quiet lake.

In 1853 Herman Melville spoke of a scene in the Berkshire Hills that I know well. "My eyes ranged over the capacious rolling country, and over the village and over a farmhouse here and there, and over woods, groves, streams, rocks, fells—and I thought to myself, what a slight mark, after all, does man make on this huge great earth." In the same spot now is a settling pond for town sewage, surrounded by discarded junk. Melville also described nearby Balance Rock, and I went to see it. It was almost completely covered with names, initials, graffiti, and vulgar words. I scraped off what I could and then descended the trail, recalling Melville's wonder at the rock's balance. "Beside…one obscure minute point of contact, the whole and enormous mass touched not another object in this whole terraqueous world."

My love affair with the American countryside began less than fifty years ago, yet very little of what I knew then remains untouched or unspoiled. But I am thankful for having known it, and glad that I can recollect bits of it and pass them on; such is the gratifying privilege of being writer and painter.

I remember being inspired first by the landscapes painted by George Inness. I especially liked his words of thankfulness "for having lived in a land of reverent agriculturists and being able to capture the mood for the future." And, he wrote, "Some persons suppose that a landscape has no power to communicate human sentiments, but that is a great mistake."

It is a shocking comment on our times that a leading advertising executive was applauded for asserting, "Billboards are the art gallery of the American public." General Outdoor Advertising further comments, "The right to communicate visually would seem to be one of our essential freedoms." One industrial spokesman has said, "The ability of a river to absorb sewage is one of America's great natural resources."

There are those who have developed an exquisite taste for devastation—who see more cultural excitement in a busy shopping center than in the quiet countryside it has replaced; who see beauty in the color and aura of garbage, and even see artistic symbols of life in waste and disharmony. Some paint and write about filth and confusion and find a ready market, but count me as one who cannot accept such reasoning. Ashcan art reflects an ashcan life.

I believe there is hope for at least a partial survival of the original America, but I cannot see this occurring without a national revolution of indignation. As free people we have a powerful capacity for righteous indignation, and since the American Revolution, it has never been more needed than right now. Therefore the following pages were indeed designed to spread alarm—without being frantic—but they are also intended to lead you to share my quiet recollections of certain things that have vanished from our heritage, of how I remember America. That is what this book is about.

Eric Sloane
Cornwall Bridge
Connecticut

Remembering

TRUE ART, IN MANY WAYS, IS THE PORTRAYAL OF remembrances.

At once I can see those who disagree pointing a finger at me. "Obsolete! True art, true genius is essentially something that has never been done before!" But these people are confusing art with *inventiveness,* and man can invent both good things and bad things, ugliness or beauty. Many art galleries nowadays are showing the work of good and bad *inventors* instead of the work of artists. This is, in fact, the age of inventors.

Inventing for the sake of inventing or creating for the sake of creating has a certain madness about it more disturbing than intelligent. It seems to me that art should be the result of having lived and thought, and should be no more accidental than God's creativity. But then as Mark Twain mused, man himself was created at the end of the week's work, when God was quite tired.

The artist, it seems to me, is usually one who writes or paints or acts or creates in his own way, but with the greatest *remembrance.* I have often found myself painting in a vague or uninspired manner until one brush stroke (perhaps an accidental movement) kindled or loosened a color, a mood, or a spirit that had been stored away in the attic of my mind. Perhaps it was a sudden flash of sunlight on the grain of ancient barn wood; perhaps I experienced this yesterday, or it might have been forty years ago. But remembering this tiny event always

evokes sufficient pleasure and inspiration enough to build all the rest of my recollections around it, so that what I paint will be a bit less of a pictorial design than an instant of my past remembrance.

The idea of building a whole painting around one inspired remembrance may be an idiosyncrasy of my own, but an artist acquires many eccentricities while groping for individual expression. I have a superstition (or is it a religious belief?) that involves prayer. I believe that the creative artist is constantly praying while working; asking for the right choice of color, the ability to portray, the correct line, what to eliminate or what to add. And I consider these mental requests as instantaneous, tiny yet true prayers. Whenever a tube of paint falls, for example, or I drop a brush with paint on it, I automatically consider this an answered prayer and find myself called upon to use that very color immediately. Insanity, superstition, or whatever, it has served me well.

The painting an artist chooses to make is often less a design or a picture than it is a piece of his own life or a longing in his own heart. That is what makes it a work of art for the beholder. I recently met a man who had bought one of my paintings some years before. "I was walking down the avenue," he told me, "with a more or less blank mind, certainly in no mood for buying a painting. As I passed a gallery window, out of the corner of my eye I saw a dusty road winding past a group of abandoned farm buildings.

It was one of your paintings, and it brought back a wonderful moment of my life that occurred so many years ago that it should have been lost in the passage of time." Of course he thought he had bought my painting, but I know for certain that what he really bought was a second or two of his own cherished youth. I'd sold a remembrance.

Some sudden stillness before a storm, some flash of sunlight on rippling water, the heavy quiet of some decaying building, the nostalgic mood of a by-gone autumn; thousands of lightning-short pictures like these are indelibly imprinted on everyone's mind, waiting to be revived by music or writing or painting, even by odors. What a picture reflects is usually the essence of its art. Ruskin was more emphatic: "You will never love art," he said, "till you love what she mirrors better." Painting to me, is not a "creative art" at all, but a recreative art or a "mir-ror-art." The so-called creative arts, it seems, are all misnamed. He who invents, weaves, builds a house or creates anything new is the creative artist; music, dance, theater, writing and painting involve not cre-ation as much as reflection.

I have found that remembrance occurs best when no effort is involved. I've often tried hard to recall something, only to fail; then later, while putting my attention on another matter, the remembrance pops up clearly as if from nowhere. That same thing often happens when an author sits down to a blank sheet of paper with the firm commitment to write: ideas just won't evolve; then later, and without effort, ideas cascade forth. Most of my writings (and paintings too) were inspired while I was operating an auto-bile, raking a lawn, remodeling a barn, or building a stone wall; that's when the ideas took shape. It is really more exciting and rewarding to work that way, for although my later writing or painting may be forgotten, I *have*, at least, built a stone wall.

I can seldom recall what I did last week or even yesterday; yet casual remembrances of many years ago often return to me as bright and as clearly framed as on the occasion when they were first ex-perienced. Surely the sun of yesterday was no more brilliant, the winds no fresher, nor the moments more profound; yet such is the illusion. Perhaps it is that peculiar phenomenon of distance which makes things viewed from afar appear more precise or even magnified. How large the rooms of my youth were as I remembered them, and how disappointingly small they really were when I visited them years later! Perhaps it is akin to a painter stepping back from his work and squinting at it in order to obtain a richer and more concise view.

It is interesting to me that so-called modern art is seldom enhanced by the squinting procedure. I tried it once in a museum of modern art, with a "white on white" canvas and the curator, who chanced by, seemed amused by my antics. "You don't have to squint that way at this kind of art," he said. "This is a forthright declaration; it has no artificial embellishments to hide its feeling."

"Sorry," I said, "I'm at a loss to see any meaning in it at all. But I guess I'm old-fashioned and too accustomed to traditional art."

I could see I had pained him. "Why must it have a meaning?" "This is an art of *now*," he said, "with-out any influence from yesterday's tradition or con-cern for tomorrow's needs. It is a pure abstract ex-pression, a happening! There is no thought here of the past or concern for the future. Why must any-thing have a *meaning?*"

I'd heard this argument before, but now it was

particularly deplorable. Art "without any influence from yesterday's tradition" or "concern for tomorrow's needs" must indeed reflect an unthinking and dangerous culture. Life without tradition can only produce art without memory; both suffer from amnesia.

I suppose as I stood there, squinting and looking for rationalism, I must have appeared out of date. Yet no man with a conscience, I thought, can live in a world of *now*, in a world without reason and meaning. Ignoring the past and the future is not civilized.

Those who have lost sight of their past are condemned to relive it, and it seems that this rule, according to history, applies to nations as well as to individuals. Living only in the *past* produces the disease of nostalgia; living only in the *present* produces irresponsibility; living only in the *future* is impossible because the future is yet to be. The real art of living, I believe, is blending equally the past, present, and concern for the future. And real art, it seems to me, should reflect this principle.

The artist who paints for a living seldom has the time to ponder the intricacies of recognition. He ignores it usually, until it is too late. Sometimes recognition arrives after his death. Perhaps if I had it all to do over, I would not paint some five miles of pictures as I did during the past half century, allowing them to sell at "reasonable prices." Yet my regard for hard work and individual accomplishment allows me to feel no regret or shame; I've given some pleasure to many people, and that might well be one very important purpose of the painter's existence.

Whatever I learned in art schools had little or nothing to do with the application of paint or the creation of pictures; it came from watching others paint and hearing what they had to say. I remember that Thomas Hart Benton insisted, "An art school is a place for young girls to pass the time between high school and marriage." I heartily agree with him.

When I was a young art student in New York City I was privileged to sit at a luncheon table with George Luks and John Sloan while they discussed recognition. "If only a young painter might work for twenty-five years or so, learning and improving his style, but using an assumed name and selling just for expenses," observed Luks. "Then after he felt his work was really ready, he could start anew with his true name, increasing his price tenfold...perhaps that would be an answer. So many painters at middle age find themselves haunted by the inferior work of their youth. Some of my own early work sickens me!" John Sloan laughed. "Just last week," he said, "I bought one of my earlier sketches from a collector, only for the purpose of destroying it. A good idea might be to work the required time without signing your name at all. Or to destroy all of your early work, as fast as you do it."

I didn't forget that conversation and I thought a lot about it during the next week of art classes. Perhaps I could work under an assumed name until my work satisfied me completely! Anyway, my real name, Everard Jean Hinrichs, was a difficult name for people to remember. Most everyone pronounced the Dutch name "Hinrichs" like the German "Heinrich," and those were the strained postwar years when anything German was unpopular. Why not a simple name like "Eric Sloan"?

I did a quick sketch of Luks and Sloan at the table and I signed it "Eric Sloan." Then, just to be different, I added an "e" to the "Sloan." It looked fine. Where the "Eric" came from, I don't recall; but I remember being pleased that it was the middle four letters of the word "American," and so I kept it.

I really intended to use the assumed name of Eric Sloane only until my painting reached some point of perfection. But in time I learned that no painter of worth is ever satisfied; I have yet to do a piece of work which couldn't in some way be improved. I am still, thank God, a student, dissatisfied with my work, and I still sign it "Eric Sloane."

I shall always feel I received some sort of heritage from John Sloan and I apologize for having added the "e." But now that I have earned an N.A. to add to the name, I feel better about it; I've even stopped wondering about ever returning to my real name of Everard Jean Hinrichs. Secretly, I'm afraid that should I go back to that name, I'd fall into dust like a mummy that has been preserved only by being protected from the air of the outside world.

Like John Sloan, I have often been haunted by samples of my early work. One sketch that I gave to a waiter as a tip during the lean years came back to me many years later when I found it in a gallery and bought it. Painted on Masonite board, it made a bright and strange flame in my fireplace, and I felt much better for having burned it. I still buy back my early works (if the prices are right) for the sole purpose of destroying them.

Somehow or other I have always detested the idea of keeping samples of one's work. I've known so many art students who "just happen to have a portfolio of sketches" with them, and who "would really enjoy a criticism." I'm sure if you carry your early work around with you long enough, you will finally fall in love with it, but to me, the idea is a bit like carrying around some old candy from a cooking school class and asking chefs to taste it and pass on its merits. My advice to any art student is to paint fast

and furiously, and then sell, hide, or destroy everything done during the first ten years. In my case I wish it had been forty years.

I was born into a home of the least artistic taste. Decoration consisted of a plaster-cast bust of Abraham Lincoln and two wall plaques of matching Indian heads; there was an oak-framed duo of lithochromed "Cupid Awake" and "Cupid Asleep"; and on the wall behind an overstuffed couch there was a long, narrow print of a foxhunt with a frame that included a horse's bit and an imitation riding crop. I was probably reborn when I left home and began thinking for myself.

One advantage of my having been raised in an inartistic family was that no one accused me of having talent; that sort of thing often frightens otherwise creative children into becoming business people. Discovering your own ability or reason for being is one of the rare and inspiring privileges of life, a deeply moving and a necessarily personal experience.

It is wearisome and even painful for an artist to be told he has talent for he, more than anyone else, is aware of what talent really is. He knows that just as anyone can walk or talk, anyone can write or paint—the only stumbling block is the inability to think correctly. A truly talented person is merely one who has an unusual ability to think, and talent is within everyone's power.

If you have awareness, sensitivity, and the ability to think, you are already an artist: I am convinced that artists are neither born into a particular world nor blessed with a unique spark. Thomas Edison was perhaps being modest when he said, "Genius is one percent inspiration and ninety-nine percent perspiration." but in my opinion, these words are a perfect definition of talent.

From 1920 to 1970.....

ANYONE WHO HAS GAINED A NAME IN HIS FIELD OF work sometimes finds that he has created an outside personality he is expected to rival. A painter who eavesdrops at his own showing soon learns about this. "Sloane does a painting in only one or two hours," said a lady at one of my shows. "At that rate," said her friend, "he could do four or five a day. Think how many he does in a year!"

Another asked, "Did you ever hear of Eric Sloane before?" Her companion shrugged his shoulders. "Of course," he said, "but he really isn't that good."

As Everard Jean Hinrichs looks back on half a century of Eric Sloane, he thinks it has all been worth the while. A painter or a writer—more than most craftsmen—is blessed with the opportunity of being himself. Builders, actors, merchants, designers, and businessmen cannot work truly alone, and must swing with the uncertain pendulum of their time and with all its changing fads. But the painter, who usually cannot escape from himself, spends half his life developing a personal theme and uses the other half expressing it.

Painting and poetry are such similar arts that I've often wondered why painters have not more often tried their hands at poetry. My most recent attempt was while I was writing *A Reverence for Wood,* and was seeking an appropriate poetic quotation for the beginning of each chapter. After searching in vain for a few lines about wood, and having a printer's deadline to meet, I decided to let Everard Hinrichs do the job for me, and thereby quoted myself. "His" poem was:

> The heft and feel of a well-worn handle,
> The sight of shavings that curl from a blade;
> The logs in the woodpile, the sentiment of huge
>   beams in an old-fashioned house;
> The smell of fresh-cut timber and the pungent
>   fragrance of burning leaves;
> The crackle of kindling and the hiss of burning
>   logs.
> Abundant to all the needs of man, how poor the
>   world would be
> Without wood.

I've had several letters asking who this unknown poet was, and two magazines asked permission to use the poem. Perhaps I should have been a poet instead!

The first attempts at painting by Eric Sloane were simple department-store posters. There were a few more ambitious assignments on brick walls, shop windows, awnings, and truck bodies. I had already learned the wonders of lettering from a neighbor whose business it was to design typefaces; Fred Goudy was a kind man who tolerated a young neighbor watching over his shoulder. He told me how he had actually traced letters carved into the stones of the Roman Forum. I watched him adapt these rough tracings into giant drawings of the alphabet which soon would become the typeface known as Goudy Forum. He even allowed me to turn the ancient handpress in his basement studio on Deepdene Street in Forest Hills, Long Island, and I printed proofs of typefaces that would later be known as Goudy Deepdene. His reverence for fine lettering was infectious, and when as a young boy I started out into the world to make my own way, it was natural that I should choose to be an itinerant sign painter.

Walking and hitchhiking from coast to coast with a kit of paints strapped to my shoulders was not the most dignified manner in which to begin an art career. Neither was the schooling derived from the painting of signs on butcher shops and oil trucks and toilet doors. But it worked for me. The free swing of arm necessary to "brush in" a big Bull Durham highway sign or to make the ten-foot letters atop the Steeplechase Amusement Park roller coaster at Coney Island gave me confidence and sureness of stroke that I still know. Lettering signs in the little cow towns of Arizona or on the café windows of New Orleans' Vieux Carré added something, too. After all, the making of an artist is far from being just the transferring of paint from a tube to a canvas. Instead, I am sure, it is being mechanic, traveler, laborer, researcher, historian, and, most of all, observer. It really amuses me when anyone asks, "How long did it take you to paint that picture?" Most of the paintings I do now began thirty or forty years ago: putting the paint from the tube to the canvas may take only an hour or two.

I remember Coney Island well. During the winter months it was a vast and tawdry fairyland with deserted cardboard castles of wonder. Although I'd gone there in the summer to paint signs at Luna Park and Steeplechase Amusement Park, I found more interest in sketching the strange mood of a carnival place closed for the season. My first big job was to paint a thousand-foot mural for Luna Park Ballroom, and I considered six hundred dollars fair pay for a young fellow. While I was working at that job, a frequent visitor—with his drawing pad—was Reginald Marsh, whose ability to sketch the amusement-park scene in red crayon was inspiring to me. "Black," he said, "really isn't a color at all. If you must use it, alizarin red with a touch of Prussian blue makes something much blacker than black." I've never owned a tube of black paint since.

Another trick Marsh showed me was the use of a nearly dry brush. Each time before applying paint, he would wipe his brush almost dry and then use a scrubbing motion to apply the color. To this day I've followed that technique, wearing out from five to ten brushes on every painting. As for rags, they have become a most important part of my equipment. Friends who know my regard for rags still send them to me for Christmas and birthdays. They are usually washed and ironed pieces of old sheets, and I couldn't expect a better gift; a few less aesthetic friends send me worn-out work pants or shirts or ladies' underwear, but I could never get into the spirit of creating with such disturbing material.

Coney Island, as I knew it, was quite different from what it is now. Doing the then new Half Moon Hotel's murals ended my sign-painting career; but I still remember how, while I worked on the hotel's Aviation Room mural, Wiley Post himself spent hours on my scaffold, helping me get down the exact details of his plane, the *Winnie Mae* (now at the Smithsonian). That was when flying the Atlantic was the great American sport. The longest airplane run-

This painting is a duplicate of a twelve-foot high mural I did with large house-painting brushes in about three hours time. I painted it for the now long-gone Inn at Roosevelt Field in Long Island. Now a vast shopping center, Roosevelt Field was the last of America's old-time flying fields. Where Lindbergh's Spirit of St. Louis took hold of the air that would carry it to Paris, there is now a Macy's department store. Where Kelly and Macready lifted off for the first non-stop transcontinental flight, there is a skyscraping bank building. Today there is nothing left there to record the days of America's colorful private flying.

way at the time was at Floyd Bennett Field in Brooklyn, and the nearest hotel to that was the Half Moon at Coney Island; so it was there that all the great flyers headquartered. Most of those transoceanic planes were lettered or numbered by me; some had an American flag or other individual emblem on the fuselage. My work on a plane came to be considered a lucky charm, and fliers such as Roscoe Turner and Bill Odom flew into Floyd Bennett Field just to have me do it. When I missed an appointment to letter de Pinedo's Transatlantic plane and it crashed on takeoff, the superstition seemed confirmed.

I remember singer Harry Richman's big single-engined Vultee. Worried about landing in the sea, he had filled its wings with ping-pong balls to keep it afloat. He came to me one day with a scrap of paper upon which he had written the words *Lady Piece*. "What I want on my plane," he said, "is this wording with crossed British and American flags underneath." Harry, I had learned, just wasn't a good speller, but I did exactly as he ordered. Luckily, after I'd painted this on the fuselage, some aircraft workers at Newark Airport accidentally used a gasoline rag to polish the plane, and smeared my lettering. I redid the sign, taking it upon myself to change the word "piece." And when the ship finally flew the Atlantic, piloted by Dick Merrill, it had the corrected name of *Lady Peace*.

It was Wiley Post who first interested me in the idea of painting the sky. On practice robot flights in the *Winnie Mae* he would sometimes take me along; with his one eye he would pick out the wonders of clouds and explain the mechanics of weather. "Some day," said Wiley, "a fellow will come along and paint nothing but the sky itself. Where else can you find higher mountains? Look at that cumulonimbus over

The Winnie Mae.

yonder—twice the height of the Matterhorn and twice as beautiful. Where else but up here could you see a better landscape of clouds?"

"What you mean is a *cloudscape*," I said. "And I wouldn't be surprised if the first fellow to try painting cloudscapes turns out to be me."

My first cloudscape was a painting of the thunderhead I saw that day from the *Winnie Mae*, and I hung it in the Roosevelt Field Inn (that old airport is now a vast shopping center). The canvas was a menacing portrayal of a cumulonimbus such as few people other than flyers had ever seen. I felt certain no one would wish to buy so dread and mysterious a picture, so I put a "For Sale" tag on it with what I thought was an outlandish price. But someone who was familiar with the subject did buy it: a check arrived from a Miss Amelia Earhart.

The experience of looking *down* at the clouds was a brand-new twentieth-century happening; yet since I first coined the word "cloudscape" nearly fifty years ago, few painters have chosen to paint that scene. With plains more vast than those on earth, mountains that would dwarf the Alps, and canyons as much as two miles deep, the cloudscape can be a powerfully moving subject.

I remember my first business card. It identified me as an "aviation artist." People with enough money to own their own planes had the money to buy paintings of them, so business was good. But as time went by, the sky took up more room in my pictures and the airplanes became tinier, until I was finally content to paint just plain sky. People would ask, "Where's the plane?" Or my friends would say, "You mean you paint *clouds*—just plain sky?" That *did* it. I had chanced upon the career with the least competition—I would be a sky painter!

My decision to paint the sky prompted me to learn first what the sky was all about. And the best way to learn, I decided, was to write a book about it. At least that was my way, so I began writing. I called that first book *Clouds, Air and Wind*, and the fact that I was actually learning meteorology while I wrote about it turned out to be doubly valuable, for later the reader learned the subject along with me. "You don't talk down to your audience" was the comment of the Army Air Force when they accepted the book as a weather manual. "It is almost as if you were learning the subject as you wrote the book," they said. How right they were!

Five more books about weather followed. I even tried my hand at being the first weatherman on TV, but I still didn't feel I had become a master of skyscapes. I remember going to the American Museum of Natural History in New York. "What do you have here about the atmosphere?" I asked. "I want to learn more about the sky." The guard didn't think there was any such exhibit, but he sent me to the curator's office.

"This isn't an aviation museum," I was told. "We have nothing at all on meteorology. Our exhibits are entirely confined to natural history."

I reminded him that all natural history happens to be confined to atmosphere—that the moon has no natural history simply because it lacks atmosphere. "The most important thing you should have here," I said, "is a Hall of Atmosphere." The curator's attitude made me feel unwelcome. "Sorry, young fellow," he said curtly, "we are limited in funds at the present time. Therefore we do not contemplate any new displays like that. Good day."

"I still think you should have a Hall of Atmosphere," I insisted. "I'll see if I can find you the money to build one." And I left. I'm sure they were glad to be rid of me.

I then went to a neighbor of mine, William Willetts, and told him about my problem. "I'd like you to introduce me to your friend Trubee Davison, who's the head of the museum and seems to be quite a man. I think I can interest him in a Hall of Atmosphere." Bill heard me out. "I have an even better idea," he said. I've been wanting to create some sort of memorial for my son Prentice who was killed in an air crash. Why don't I donate the money for your Hall of Atmosphere?" We shook hands on it.

Bill transformed his squash court into a studio workshop, and I began building three-dimensional models of weather phenomena. Our little company needed a weather-sounding name but I never liked the ancient misleading word *meteorology* which started when people thought meteors caused the weather. So I invented the word *airology* (which has since become a proper scientific word) and "Airology Workshop" became a busy little factory. There were soon Plexiglas cold and warm fronts and tornadoes and hurricanes. Lightning flashed, winds blew, and simulated rain fell from plastic clouds. I wanted movement in the displays, so I used those circular fans I had seen in artificial fireplaces (the heat of an electric light bulb turns tiny fins to create the illusion of flickering flames). Within a year or so the Willetts Memorial was installed in the museum as the very first Hall of Atmosphere anywhere.

But that was long ago. The fiber clouds soon turned black from the impurities in New York's air, and the fan-light motion was later replaced by electric-motor-driven illumination effects. I suppose if I went back to see my brainchild now, I would find it quite different from the original.

During my study of weather, I started a collection of early American diaries, because they always contained daily weather accounts full of rich lore and quaint descriptions of sky conditions. The fascination of reading these accounts of older times soon proved to influence me in other directions, and before long my paintings were depicting more Americana and less meteorology. Whereas I used to add a tiny barn or farm building to give further identity to a cloudscape, I was now using a touch of sky merely to enhance more elaborate farm scenes.

I once set up a camera to capture a particular storm cloud that I thought might make a good subject for a painting. Several people stopped to watch, all of them staring off into the distance, seeing nothing but sky and wondering what I was up to. "I don't get it," someone said. "What are you photographing?" I suppose we are so accustomed to the panorama of sky that we are not aware of its definite anatomy. Even art schools, which teach how to draw and paint everything from still-life subjects to trees and animals, have seldom touched upon the important subject of sky. About twenty years ago I did the first sky book for art students and called it *Skies and the Artist*. But even now, though the major portion of so many great paintings consists of sky, there is still little or no instruction available on the painting of clouds and the heavens.

One of the secrets of painting sky and clouds is to ignore outlines and to concentrate instead on solid masses of light and solid masses of shade. I use one large house-painting brush for the light and another equally large brush for the shade; then smaller brushes may be used for finishing. By working first with these enormous brushes, I accumulate the primary masses and shapes quickly, without outlines,

seventy feet

Size is always a challenge to the painter who, if he cannot paint the best, might at least manage to paint the biggest. Many years ago I offered to the Smithsonian Institution in Washington the gift of a cloudscape. Now they recently accepted the offer with a footnote that the painting should be seven stories high! It seems that the new building (Air and Space Museum) finds use for such a mural and it must also be about seventy feet long. Having not yet learned to say "no" and with the secret wonder of how I shall manage to get up there, as this edition goes to press your author will probably be defying his age of over seventy by painting the world's biggest cloudscape, seven stories high. This is the actual first sketch for that mural, done on the back of a restaurant place mat for astronaut Michael Collins, director of the museum.

and often do a skyscape in amazingly little time. I recollect doing one large mural for the then new Morton Salt Building in Chicago: the subject, much to my pleasure, was to be a cloud-filled sky. Using a garbage-pail lid as a palette and a number of stock house-painting brushes, I started the job at nine in the morning. By noon I had finished, and by the time the president of the company arrived to see me begin the job, I was on a plane back to New York. There are still those who value art only by the time its creation takes, but the president of Morton Salt, Daniel Peterkin, was an honest man with a sense of humor; he paid me the price we had agreed on, and even kept the garbage-pail-lid palette as a memento.

Although art is not valued by the pound or by the area it covers, certain people (even a few galleries) seem to have that impression; hardly a week goes by without some request for smaller paintings. "Some folks can't afford the price that your big paintings bring," I've been told. "Do paint some *smaller* pictures." One friend dropped by with a frame about one-inch square. "When you have a moment or two," he said, "I'd like you to dash off a little painting for my daughter's doll house."

The size equation of art values is interesting. I made a study of it and found that as some painters age, they often use smaller dimensions; also there have been cycles of both giant paintings and miniatures. The largest known painting in America is John Banvard's "Panorama of the Mississippi" (completed in 1846), painted on a twelve-foot-high strip nearly three miles long. The largest painting in existence, I understand, is the "Battle of Atlanta"—a four-hundred-foot cyclorama weighing nine tons. It was the Hudson River School that introduced wall-sized landscapes in Americana; but as windows grew bigger and wall spaces grew smaller during the last century, paintings diminished too. I insist that a large painting can be appropriate for a tiny room because it can (like a window) cause a wall to seem to recede or even to disappear.

I suppose I have always been influenced by the Hudson River School because it specialized in bringing together the mood of the American landscape and the sky. Bierstadt, Moran, Inness, Church, Kensett, Cole, Durand, and all those who portrayed the American scene with such reverence, painted with this purpose. They all lived to see their work honored, and accepted as Americana, but soon afterward they were replaced by painters whose main objective seemed to be the art of being different.

The revolt against realism and "academic monopoly" came to a head in 1913 when the famous "Eight" organized the Armory Show in New York City to honor any and all "ism" schools of painting. I guess it was a good revolution, for no one was killed; but the old-style academicians weakened and died natural deaths in nostalgic bohemias and dreary attic studios.

The good new school of modern art pushed its foot solidly into the public's door, and the door has unfortunately never been closed since, open to blob schools, all-black canvases, paper cutouts, soup tins, and plastic hamburgers. Someone discovered that shock and fad not only sell, but are respected.

The only one who has really suffered from the art revolution, it seems, is the man on the street; he is still as confused as he was at the Armory Show in 1913. The powers-that-be today—those galleries that are more apt to sell prestige than art, and the critics whose abstract rhetoric conjures a holy and fashionable awe—seldom agree with the man on the street;

Forgive the intrusion of the airplane and let me explain.

Placing an airplane in a cloudscape, I suppose, makes a piece of potential easel art just an illustration, or what the critics would call "commercial." Yet pop art of tomato soup cans and plaster bathroom seats manages to be accepted! The tiny plane in this skyscape however, has more than illustrative value, for it informs the viewer of the size of the clouds. The painters of the Hudson River school seldom failed to include a person or familiar object in their towering landscapes, and the effect was to measure a vastness of space. I remember learning this from a teacher at Yale. "Take a blank sheet of paper and look at it," he said. "It portrays little or no size. Then put a tiny pencil dot in the center and suddenly the space around it grows to a large and definite proportion." So when I do a large cloudscape (I've done some as large as thirty feet in length), I feel it is no desecration of art when I add a plane-shaped dot. Even if it is too small for most people to notice immediately, it gives me a certain satisfaction.

some smile tolerantly at him, others turn their backs. Yet this ridiculed man, who claims to know nothing about art, who "only knows what he likes," is a man of the utmost worth. His opinion deserves recognition because culture is never the product of only a special few. He will be the first to admit to being a mere child in the school of "isms," but blessed are all "men on the street" for they are truly of the kingdom of art. I am proud to be a member of that group.

I have always enjoyed gallery-owner Victor Hammer's definition of modernism in art. Victor, who uses parables deliciously, tells of a shipload of sardines that was sold and resold a dozen times, and with each sale the price of the cargo skyrocketed. Finally, realizing that no one had ever tasted the sardines, the current owner of the shipload opened a can, tasted a fish, and spat it out. "Phooey!" he said, "these sardines are not for eating—they're just for buying and selling!" Victor insists modern art is often like that.

I am of the opinion that the strange and unintelligible art generally called modern cannot possibly represent American culture, since it is not understood by the average American. Emerson said: "Culture is one thing and varnish another." When shall we learn that "culture," like the kingdom of heaven, lies entirely within us, in the heart of the national soul, and not in galleries or books?

As music is the poetry of Sound,
So is painting the poetry of Sight.

J.A. Whistler

I remember the Sky

IT WOULD ONCE HAVE SOUNDED PREPOSTEROUS TO SAY man could ever change the sky, yet he has; unfortunately, he managed to place his disturbing marks on it. There is seldom a completely unmarred sky nowadays, a sky without some confusion of jet condensation trails. This, however, is only a slight sample of what tomorrow's sky will be like, for the planned high-altitude (65,000 feet or over) transports will be leaving trails too lofty for quick disintegration; instead, they could remain in orbit for as long as two years, accumulating or even enlarging.

I suppose the day will arrive when a painting

showing a normal sky will be considered antique folk art. Painter Robert Kuhn, known for his pictures of wildlife, found contrails so much a part of the African sky that he frequently included them in his paintings. It is strange to see lions or giraffe in settings of some of the world's last untouched landscape, while the whole sky is crisscrossed with man's rude interference.

Oxygen has little weight, but each jet trail you see represents the burning of tons of this element that is so essential to life. A transatlantic jet burns about thirty-five tons, adding greatly to the increasing scarcity of oxygen. Air pollution is a moral as well as an economic issue: reason says destroying clean air is impractical; faith says it is suicidal and hence sinful.

Time was when the sky was continually clear and the air was fresh with oxygen aplenty. I was only a small boy when I first noticed the difference between city air and country air. The first nights of summer vacation were always spent in sound sleep; waking in the morning, breathing in quarts of country air, was an astonishing tonic. The carbon monoxide and sulphur dioxide in the air today make yesterday's fresh air only a remembrance. Thirty years from now, this deadly condition of city air will be twenty-five percent worse; at that rate it will take only a century or so for the air to become like that in a closed garage in which an automobile engine has been running. There are reliable biologists who predict that life on earth will finally end in a struggle for breath, a process that has already begun.

The word "weather," which started out to mean simply "the state of the atmosphere," has now become a bad word—we "brave the weather" and "protect ourselves against the weather." Rain, which used to be regarded as a blessing, is now considered more of a nuisance. I recollect when people walked in the rain for the joy of it. Fog was fascinating; drizzle was relaxing; wind was exhilarating. That was when there were verandas to sit on at night, when people watched the sunset, twilight, dusk, and moonrise; these heavenly backdrops, designed for our daily doings, are almost unnoticed now.

I can't forget the childhood evenings I spent on the long porch of our summer place. As night took over, we would light sticks of fragrant punk to drive away the flying insects. The burning sticks created a series of tiny, gyrating crimson lights as the ladies swayed back and forth in their rocking-chairs, and father's cigar was a larger and less active light at the far end of the porch. Just before blackness the trees became strange shapes against the sky, and we would make a game of picking out silhouettes that looked like Indian heads, or dragons, or animal forms. There were always shapes like that in the sky, too; sometimes the clouds resembled castles and often they would be outlined by distant heat lightning.

Nowadays we think of clouds as vaporous masses without much shape, but the old-timers were more aware of the sky. You heard a great deal about thunderheads, mackerel skies and sheep-herd clouds, anvil-tops and mares' tails. Weather lore used to be important. Not long ago the publisher of a chain of newspapers felt that weather lore was interesting enough to ask me to do a daily column about it. But his city editors turned the idea down. "We couldn't be less interested in weather lore," they said. "What the public wants to know is just one thing—will it rain tomorrow or won't it?" The old fun of philosophizing about weather is a disappearing art.

Lincoln said he could not imagine a man looking

at the sky and denying God; Emerson called the sky the daily bread of his eyes; Ruskin considered the sky almost human in its passions. From the beginning there was an awareness of the sky that has now all but gone; the spiritual feelings it once evoked are sadly missing. Poets used to refer to the sky as "the heavens," but how ridiculous it would sound today to say you flew from here to there "through the heavens." The true dictionary definition of "heavens," nevertheless, is exactly the same as "sky."

There are those who think the sky and its panoramic show were created just for the workings of weather, but the aesthetic qualities of the sky more than balance its importance as a rain and wind machine.

I find nothing as dramatic and moving as the visual music of a great storm. Each sequence unfolds with a panorama of color that matches or outdoes anything produced on earth. Cumulus clouds, which are the visible heads of rising warm-air funnels, tower and unfold so slowly that they seem to be as motionless as mountains. Yet if sped up, each cloud would grow, burst, and collapse with incredible rhythm and flowing motion.

I remember first being impressed by the magnitude of the Grand Canyon, and then mystified by its ability to change in mood and color even as I watched. While painting views of the canyon, I realized that it was really the sky that produced the constant color symphony and changed the mood; at times it even became the subject matter rather than the background or accessory to the landscape. The canyons and mountains formed of clouds, which often surpass those on earth, are with us so constantly that we seldom look at them.

The bright light of the sky causes one to squint or turn away from the upward scene, missing much of the color, but I found that observing the sky through what I call a "black glass" made it simpler for me to see sky colors. If the underside of a pane of glass is covered with black paint, the reflections on the upper side then become truer and more vivid, without any disturbing glare.

The bright sun seems to have a blinding effect on many artists who paint on location. Many western paintings are done in a pastel or almost misty effect, though the western atmosphere is really exceedingly clear—everything is either definite brightness or definite shadow. I found that first making notes or taking camera shots outdoors, then doing the finished painting indoors was my best landscape technique, rather than painting from life.

The sky, I learned, has its own (reversed) science of color and perspective. Whereas land color-perspective accentuates red in the foreground, yellow in the middleground, and blue in the distance, the nearby ceiling of sky has the most blue overhead, yellow in the middle area, and red in the distance. A painter can actually make one cloud recede behind another simply by adding to it a tinge of red; anyone may observe how the most distant clouds are always the reddest. Even white lightning, from afar, becomes red.

Clouds, which are composed of tiny mirrors (globules of condensed vapor), have the ability to reflect light, even to reflect the dullness or color of landscapes below. The bases of oceanic clouds may therefore be tinged with the greens and blues of the sea. The cloudscape, shown on page 27, reflects the blackness of the canyons below, shaded by a storm. Subject matter dances between sky and land, but the anatomy of the great storm is the more exciting.

Cumulus clouds (cloud lumps) are really visible heads of giant, rising columns of heated air (thermals) that move vertically from the sun-warmed earth. In the Far West where the sun heats arid land, thermals shoot up swiftly and burst into thunderheads of gigantic proportions, to reflect in a most subtle manner the colorings of the earth below. Moran and Innes and many landscape painters with meteorological knowledge correctly portrayed this phenomenon. Poets like Shelley, Goethe, and Saint-Exupéry were meteorologists, too.

Shelley was remarkably correct in a scientific sense when he wrote:

I am the daughter of earth and water,
    And the nursling of the sky;
I pass through the pores of ocean and shores;
    I change but I cannot die.
For after the rain with never a stain,
    The pavilion of heaven is bare,
And the winds and sunbeams with their convex gleams,
    Build up the blue dome of air,
I silently laugh at my own epitaph,
    And out of the caverns of rain,
Like child from the womb, like a ghost from the tomb,
    I arise and unbuild it again.

I remember Marshes

IT IS HARD NOWADAYS TO CREATE A MENTAL PICTURE of what a farmer looks like, but a century ago you would have had very little trouble. Even then he had lost his prominence as lord of the land, for agrarianism had already begun to collapse. The boys had come home from the Civil War, and then set out for the cities with hopes of becoming rich. And the farmer was suddenly cartooned as a bewhiskered rube—usually with a wide-brimmed hat and always with heavy boots.

The farmer and his boots were inseparable. Store shoes were only for churchgoing. The truth is that his boots were necessary, for the ground was entirely different from what we walk on today. Under the grass, not long ago, was a thick layer of mossy compost, then a foot-deep mixture of humus. Beneath that came a rich topsoil—two feet of it, and all of it was moist. When you walked across such a meadow, you squashed and bounced over a carpet of wetness that to the old-time farmer was the real wealth of his land. Yesterday was a rich, wet, different world.

The next time you motor through a cut in the countryside (where the highway has been blasted through a hill), notice that the portion of soil above rock, where the trees are growing, is now only a foot or two deep. Tree roots, therefore, can no longer burrow downward but have to spread outward only a few inches underground. Whereas trees a century ago received a good quantity of moisture from the earth, trees that have to grow in the thin and dry carpet of today's soil live almost entirely on moisture contained in the atmosphere.

The word "swamp" has become an ugly term in modern usage. Fens, bogs, marshes, ponds, and other wet spots are no longer valuable land, but rather

29

places to be filled in and covered with hardpan. Otherwise they aren't even considered real estate.

Not very long ago there was a project to get rid of America's Great Dismal Swamp to make way for a lucrative real-estate development. "After all," said one newspaper, "a swamp is useless. It represents nothing but disease and danger." These words reminded me of another article from my collection of early newspapers:

The Dismal Swamp, says one who has been there, is not a vast bog sunk low in the ground, into which all the draining of surrounding country flows; on the contrary, it is above ground some fifteen or twenty feet. It is an immense reservoir, the richest and most valuable land in the American nation. Anyone would suppose the "Dismal" was a veritable charnel house spreading its miasma throughout the country; on the contrary, it is the healthiest place imaginable. The swamp is formed of green timber; there is absolutely no decomposed wood. Trees fall prone on the ground, but instead of the wood decomposing, it turns to peat and lies indissoluble by air and water for ages, perfectly sound. All is fresh, and the air is laden with as sweet odors as the fragrance of the woods in May. The water is pure and sweet, tinged to a faint wine hue by the juniper, a potent medicinal drink.

Today, because man has robbed the land of its blotterlike quality, water drains off to the only places in which it can collect, making the valuable old ponds and marshes in America no more than ugly sinkholes and collectors of waste. The best way to fill in a sinkhole, according to modern-day thinking, is first to fill it with any available junk. And the best way to cover such a dump, in order to make it valuable, is with concrete. One such project was recently finished near my home town. It is now as vast a stretch of flat parking space as I've ever seen. "And

to think," remarked the builder proudly, "this was once just a marsh!"

I did think. I remembered a day when, in a canoe, I pushed through the reeds and flags there. Usually small boys were fishing in it. There were red-winged blackbirds and herons, and at night it was alive with the staccato music of toads and the guttural guitar responses of green frogs. "I liked it better the way it was," I said. "You," he replied firmly, "are old-fashioned!"

We are so immersed in the business of turning the earth and its riches into cash that the conservationist finds difficulty in selling his argument. Even Gifford Pinchot, the great American conservationist, left the door open to some misconception when he defined conservation as "the wise use of the earth

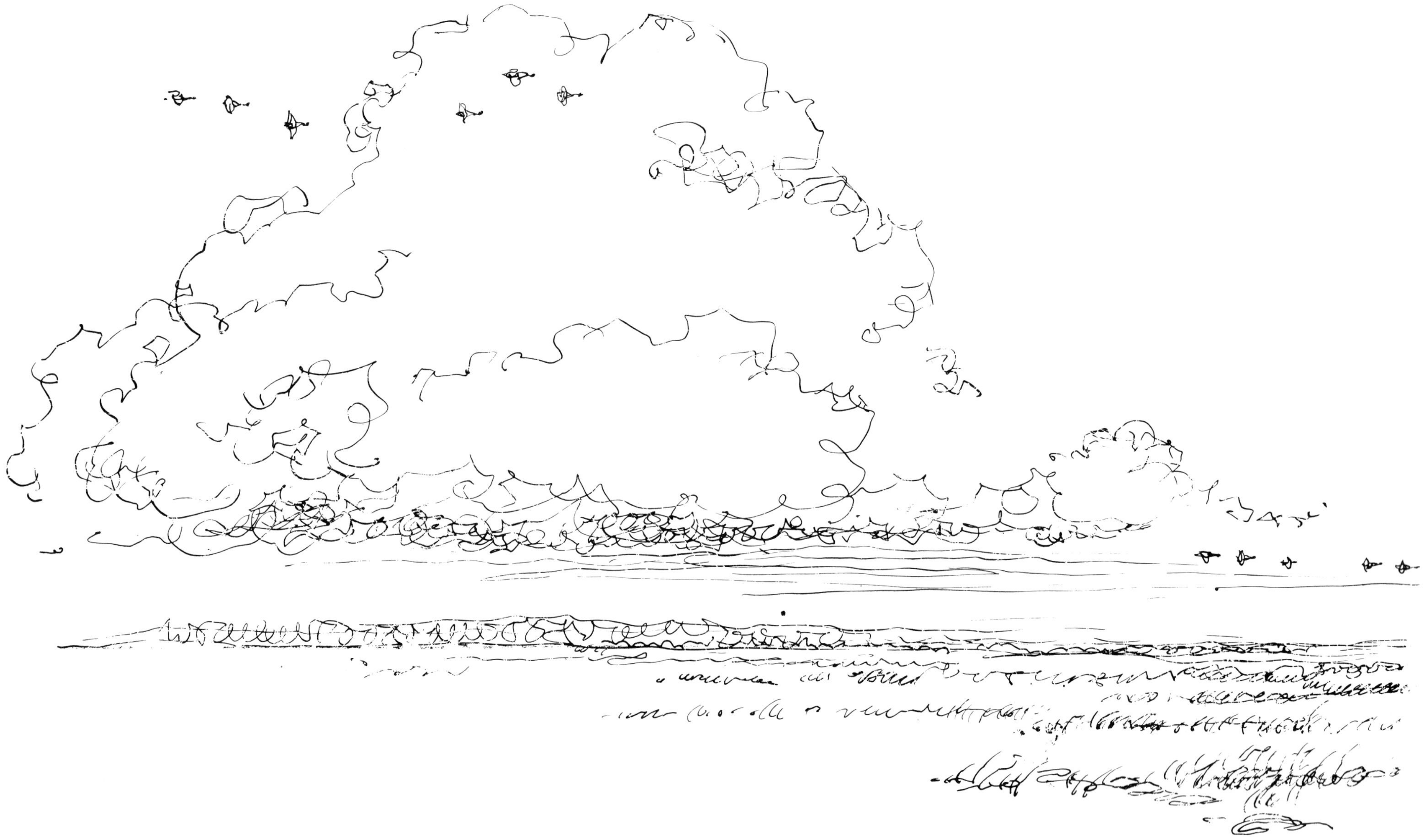

and its resources for the lasting good of men." That almost indicates that *every* bit of the earth should be used by man. And what, according to the American mind, is "for the lasting good of men" but *cash* bringing in interest? Cash that comes from such things as oil, ore, timber, gravel, or real estate. I think Pinchot should also have included "the wise *un-use* of the earth for the lasting good of man."

A marsh on this planet is regarded as a wasteland to be reclaimed, but if one marsh could be found on the moon or another planet, it would be the most valuable spot there, perhaps even the birthplace of a new civilization. Sadly, I can foresee us using most of our natural resources in attempting to reach other planets, only to realize that the other planets were not designed for our kind of living.

Here on the earth that God designed for us are all the physical and aesthetic things we need in order to live. If a man looks at a marsh and can find no beauty there, he is well on his way to ignoring his heritage, and perhaps he deserves the poverty of overdevelopment.

It is interesting that the decaying hull of an abandoned boat can be an agreeable part of a seashore or salt-marsh scene, while modern junk is always offensive. Tires or automobile bodies are certainly representative of man's genius, yet when discarded in a derelict state, one sees in them only ugliness.

This painting aims at envisioning the freshness of untouched marshland and clean air. Such scenes seem destined nowadays only for the sportman's wall, too mundane to be considered serious art. Perhaps it is because we see them so much without appreciation; at any rate, I feel no artistic guilt.

A cloudscape cannot be painted from life. Although the movement seems slow or even motionless, the sky is in a constant and magnificent process of change. The movement of a cloud from birth to disintegration resembles the life of a flower: first the budding, then a rythmical blooming, and finally a falling away into nothingness. The colors of the sky change faster than even the swiftest water-colorist could catch them.

There were roads

I FIND LITTLE-USED DIRT ROADS AN INVITATION. PERhaps some day motorists will be lucky enough to find places where, for a toll, they can travel a mile or so down a dirt lane, through shaded glens, over a clean brook on a wooden bridge, and perhaps through a quiet village. I once lived on such a road, and when company arrived, it was my custom to take everyone for a spin in my 1928 Model-A Ford depot hack. I returned home from the city one day to find the road had been tarred and the trees cut back fifty feet on both sides.

"We've fixed your road for you," said the First Selectman proudly. "You certainly have," I said sadly, "and now I'll put my place up for sale."

Comparing yesterday's roads with today's, I can foresee the banning of all pleasure cars from within twenty to thirty miles of each large city. Already during peak hours, the commuter's average is only about three or four times faster than a walk. The automobile can be as much a curse as it is a boon, and it has reached that point: it has killed more Americans than all our wars did, and has sharply reduced breatheable air. We spend on it nearly three times what we spend on education, and it has begun to crowd out man's living space. As our population grows we build vertically, but the automobile takes over horizontally: a man cannot build a house without the very real possibility of losing it to an automobile highway. Even school playgrounds are daily being turned into parking lots for buses and the cars of students and teachers. Nothing has lessened the quality of the air, the aesthetics of living, and the beauty of the American countryside more than the overuse of the automobile.

Automobiles have become so much a part of our lives that (at least to me) they have taken on a personality. Besides being pleasurable companions, they carry us from the hospital when newborn, take us to work and home again for a lifetime, provide a courting parlor for many, and even carry us to the grave. Turning in an old car for a new one is sometimes like deserting an old friend; when my car overheats or becomes strained on a long hill, I still feel for it as if there were something human to be concerned about. When I see a car covered with travel stickers, bumper cards, and slogans, with statues of saints and Smokey the Bear fastened to the dashboard, I sense embarrassment on the part of the automobile.

I know how important automobiles are; I even motor the length of my driveway to reach my mailbox each day. I figure I've spent eight solid years (close to 68,000 hours) operating about three dozen cars. I am old enough to recall running boards, solid tires, rumble seats, and putting chains on tires at the first drops of rain. And I recall also that the old cars and the old roads had a certain charm of their own.

My Packard Twin-Six and my Model-T were seven feet high, and when you toured, you had a fine view of the countryside. Now your eyes are not much higher than three feet from the gutter and the exhaust of the car ahead. It is hard to realize that when you sit in the driver's seat, your eyes are now at the same height (or below) as if you were in the road, on your knees (try that and see for yourself). Or that modern cars (even station wagons) are inches below the horizontally outstretched arm of an average man. Of course, there is less to see than there used to be, and the roadsides have become a maze of ugliness. But my memories of touring the country from an elevated position, with the windshield down (how I miss that!), are a rich segment of my past life.

As the wind blows
So goes the weather.

Gone with the wind

c. 1850

50 pounds of sheet iron... Pennsylvania 1760

THERE'S NO DOUBT ABOUT IT: ONE THING LEADS strangely to another. It seemed appropriate for me as a weatherman to collect weather vanes, so I began collecting them before they reached the expensive antique market. Even with my limited income, I managed at that time to gather enough of them to make walking about my home a problem. Finally I gave up keeping the clumsy finials with the north, east, south and west initials and just collected the decorative statuary. I recall buying one old barn (to use the siding to make frames for my paintings) for one hundred dollars; the weather vane on it had sold the week before for three hundred! It later sold to a folklore museum for three thousand dollars. Few items are as historically decorative and rich with the aura of early times as primitive weather vanes; my collection outgrew a weatherman's hobby, but it helped to spark my real interest in Americana.

When one paints farm scenes on location, surrounded by the quiet buildings of a deserted barnyard and sheltered from the sounds of an outside world, there is a stillness that often gives one a dreary feeling. You wait to hear the moving of animals inside the barn, the cluck of a chicken, or anything to break the noiselessness. I have frequently heard the comforting sound of some out-of-sight weather vane breaking the silence with faraway squeaks as it turned with the changing wind. And then I cannot help pondering about that one farm machine constantly working through the seasons and years, still calling out the weather to a now dead farm. If there is anything left to symbolize the old-time farmstead and its unchanging way of life, it may indeed be the weather vane.

More than the barometer or any other meteorological instrument, the weather vane is the prime

Other than buggy whips, I suppose carriage stones are about as obsolete a piece of Americana as one could think of. In Pennsylvania where the Conestoga and other farm wagons were particularly lofty, it was completely necessary to have such a stepping stone device for boarding and loading. There, they were called "upping blocks," and very few of them now remain intact. I sketched one upping block in Bucks County which was the same height as the top of my station wagon, and I mused how road vehicles have become lower with the years.

When I needed a hearthstone during my house remodelling, I heard of a fine five-foot granite slab which was on top of a set of carriage steps at a nearby abandoned farm. "It will be just right as a hearthstone," said my builder. "In fact it was a hearthstone before the farmer, about a century ago, used it as a carriage step." So as I sit before my kitchen fireplace, I contemplate my hearthstone turned upping-block, returned to hearthstone. The old time habit of "making use" is a most satisfying one.

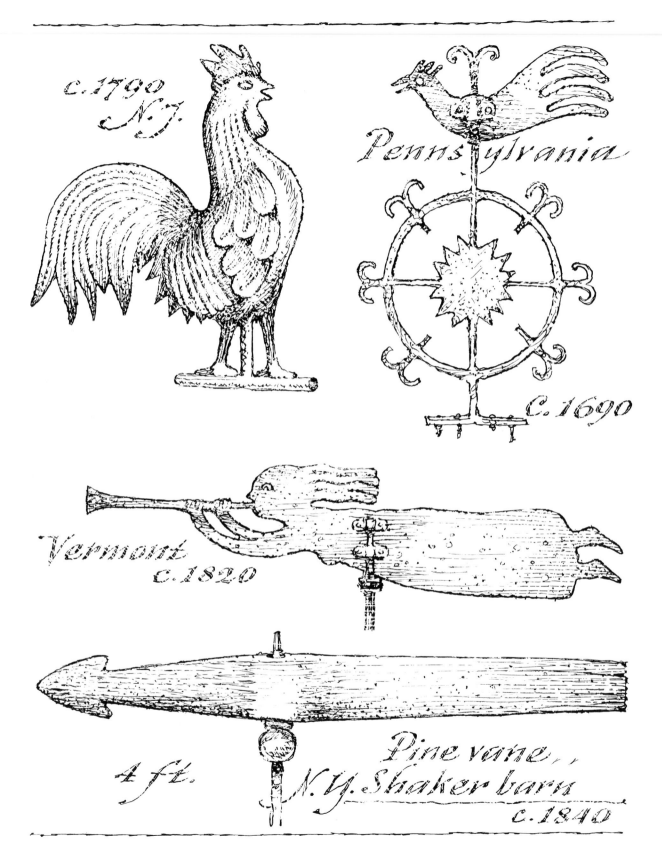

c. 1790 N.J.

Pennsylvania

c. 1690

Vermont c. 1820

4 ft.

Pine vane, N.Y. Shaker barn c. 1840

implement of weather forecasting; of first importance is the wind direction and its tendency to change by either "backing" or "veering." I have never been able to find a very early American weather vane because they were all made of light, soft wood and have, therefore, long since disappeared. The first colonists, who were deeply concerned with the vagaries and sudden changes of American weather, also used the same device they had atop their boat masts—a strip of cloth or "weather pennant." In fact the word "vane" comes from the Old English word "fana" (flag). The weather vane, as we now know it, was less a weather instrument than it was an ornament and symbol; some were so heavy that it took a strong gale to make them swing at all.

Most of the weather vanes in my collection were peppered with bullet holes, and many antique dealers will say that this is the result of "shots by Revolutionary soldiers." But vanes will swing with surprising and delightful agility when hit, and they have always been a challenge to any small boy with a rifle. I doubt if Revolutionary soldiers wasted their shots in the days of the flintlock.

At one time in France it was the custom of the nobility to top their castles with emblematic weather vanes, but after the French Revolution even the humblest cottage began sporting vanes. The stationary weathercock was a very early pagan symbol dedicated to Helios, the sun god, for the cock's unfailing service in hailing the rising sun. Later when a Papal Decree accepted the cock as a Christian emblem (associated with the repentance of Peter), most churches were topped with weathercocks—some stationary, others swinging with the wind.

Shem Drowne, a famous American weather-vane

maker, constructed a weathercock for a church built in Boston in 1720. The congregation was in revolt against its previous pastor, and the new building was nicknamed the "First Revenge Church of Christ." Shem's weathercock was called the "Revenge Cockerel." Some vowed that bad luck would result from such sacrilege, and sure enough, with the first big blow, Shem Drowne's Revenge Cockerel, being so heavy (it had been hammered from 172 pounds of old copper pots), blew down and wrecked the roof of the parsonage next door.

The collector can tell instantly, by its design and art tendencies, the age of most American weather vanes; the older the vane, the more exact he can be, even to determining the area in which it was made. Roofline Americana continues to tell the story of our times, for the homemade weather vane is gone and the television antenna has replaced it. The result is anything but an improvement to my eyes—even at the indoor end of the antenna.

My oldest weather vanes were all lacking the extended iron initials for east, west, north, and south, and I wondered if they had become lost during the years. Then I realized they were simply not necessary in those pioneer days because everyone was so completely familiar with the cardinal points of the compass. Houses and barns and even privies were built according to prevailing winds and the path of sunlight: people spoke of east or west as easily as we now refer to our right or left. One old farmhouse I bought had references in the deed to the "west field," "south marsh," and the "north rise": there was also mention of a "spring-pipe at the northeast corner of the cellar." To find that pipe necessitated several turns in getting down the cellar stairs, which always left me in the dark cellar with no sense of direction

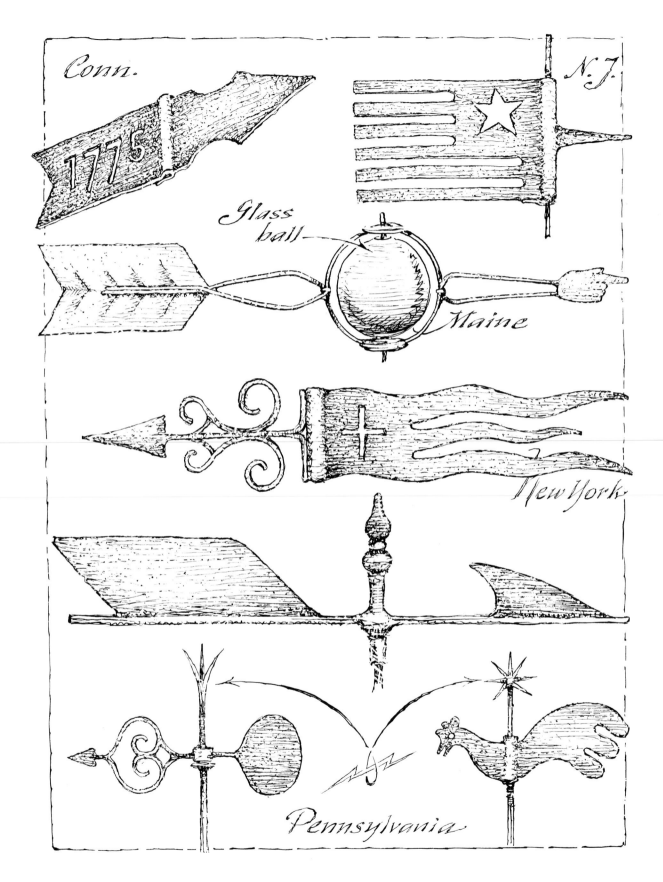

43

Painting my own barns, I find the texture of their weathered wood and the composition of their shadowed shapes gives an endless change of subject material. This painting was the one originally too large for entry in an art show. I sawed it nearly in half, and it won the Gold Medal, so I wonder if chance is not sometimes involved with success.

The gilt hand of the actual weathervane, which now hangs in my studio, points accusingly in the direction of the other half of the painting, which I have hung as a memento.

at all. Finally I had to bring a compass with me; but I'm sure the farmer who lived there a couple of centuries ago would have known "the northeast corner" blindfolded.

The Maine weather vane with a glass ball started as a combination wind vane and lightning rod. The glass ball was supposed to shatter when hit by lightning; in fact it was sold with an extra supply of glass balls. But it was soon found that lightning tends to fuse whatever it hits, so the combination rod and vane proved ineffectual and is now a rare item of Americana. The Pennsylvania combination lightning rod and weather vane, including sharp points "to attract electricity," is even rarer.

There are still half a dozen weather-vane manufacturers in the United States, but the really

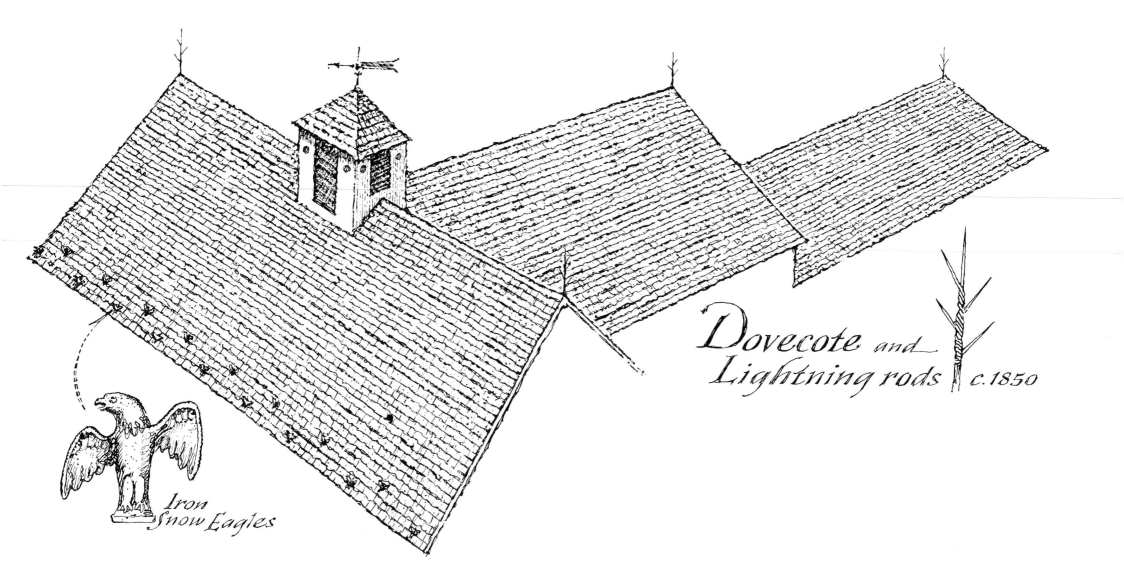

Iron Snow Eagles

Dovecote and Lightning rods c.1850

The silhouette of the ancient Hoxie House at Sandwich, Massachusetts, identifies it as having been built during colonial days. Many old houses were designed with that particularly steep pitch of roof necessary for a thatched covering; when thatching became contrary to the colonial fire laws and the custom was abandoned here, roofs on new houses had a flatter pitch.

The older houses, built for thatched roofs, have great attics, and the nearly forty-five degree slant of roof makes a high wind feed the draft of its chimney rather than force it back and downward. The situation, placement as to the points of the compass, and a thousand other things which the modern builder disregards, all went to create a unique architecture. Subtle as the physical differences may be, a new building made to resemble an ancient one cannot capture the complete feeling of antiquity.

weather-wise American has all but vanished. Houses today are built without regard to the compass, are designed only to face streets or roads instead of being in a proper weather site. The lore of sky and winds belongs to the world of long ago.

There is a typical snugness about early rural architecture that is difficult to reproduce. Part of the problem is that the overall roof was once more of a basic plan, and today it is always an afterthought. Formerly, the roof and house shape were first decided on (before any distribution of rooms); nowadays, the arrangement of rooms is the first thing to be decided, then room shapes are covered over with a roof. This leaves the house shape anything but simple. When you fly over the countryside, you can rapidly pick out all the ancient houses for they stand apart, snug and simple, in the maze of incongruous modern shapes. If you are ever out driving at about sunset, you will be amazed to discover how easy it is to identify the old houses just by their silhouettes. Playing this game one autumn evening in Massachusetts, I braked my car to a quick stop before a dramatic house shape set on a hill. Its outline gave its age as plain as if there had been words on a plaque in front of the house. "That," I said to the friend who was with me, "is surely the oldest house of all!" Indeed it was the oldest one on Cape Cod—the Hoxie House, built in 1637.

Roof ventilators, too, have nearly vanished from modern architecture, although there still exist occasional (misnamed) "cupolas," which were added for quaintness or as a base for an ornamental weather vane. A true cupola is domed and cup-shaped; the squarish American farm type is really a *ventilator* or *dovecote*. Before pesticides, birds were a beautiful accessory to the farmyard, and they were encouraged to nest on rooftops in these combination ventilator-bird barns.

Because the early Franklin lightning rods had sharp points, and many Puritans objected to "the aiming of sharp points at the Almighty," some Vermonters covered their barn lightning rods with ventilator boxes "in respect for the Lord." But it was Benjamin Franklin himself who correctly presumed that unventilated hay harbored static electricity and that a big ventilator was insurance against a barn being struck. By the early 1800s the oversize rooftop ventilator had become a standard Vermont barn architectural feature.

Some early barn builders purposely left nails protruding at random to hold a blanket of snow as insulation against the winter cold. "Snow eagles" were originally designed for this purpose but later they were placed only near the edge of the roof to keep snow from sliding off and causing injury. These little iron snow eagles, which once sold in barrel lots at five dollars a barrel, are now rare antique store items.

Roofs were very important in the early days, but now that roofs are covered with plastic linoleumlike sheets, which will last for the short life of the average house, few regard a roof as being anything other than a cover. The first-growth cedar shakes of yesterday lasted a century or more; moss and decay added to their weatherproofing qualities and, of course, to the pleasure of their beholder.

The oldest tobacco barns in Connecticut have the peculiar habit of settling into the landscape after perhaps a century, so that the roofline finally conforms with the contour of the land. Even with a twisted roof, the shingles shift and remain flat, continuing to keep out the rain.

I Remember Barns

I REMEMBER BARNS BECAUSE, AS A PAINTER OF them, that is exactly what I have *had* to do; I do not paint on location. It has always seemed to me that the best way to capture the mood of any scene is to regard it as an echo in the mind, after I have made photographs or sketches. Such a recollection at the easel is that much less photographic, more a memory and therefore more a free design.

My peculiar reputation of being "America's barn painter" has often resulted in amusing confusion. There are still those who think this title refers to some sort of house painter, and seldom does a month go by without someone whose barn needs a coat of paint requesting an estimate from "Sloane, the barn painter."

Although I regard nostalgia as a dread disease, still it is difficult to paint scenes of long ago without some reverence being evoked. Americans have been the last to find any merit whatsoever in obsolescence and even less in decay, so my audience is usually quick to be critical. One gallery asked if I would do a painting of a "better-kept barn" for a client who owned a prosperous farm and could not bear to see any farm buildings in disrepair. I also recall one buyer who brought a painting back to me, asking me to restore some of the missing boards and broken windows and to trim the overgrown grass. After all, he argued, it was exactly what I'd done to my own old barn.

I feel that when Nature is allowed to have her

This cow on the weathervane now hangs on my wall.
I found it many years ago and gave it away as a gift
to a farmer friend on his ninety-second birthday. I
thought he would use it as an ornament, but he was a
practical old dairyman who avoided ornamentation
and made it back into a weathervane. I found that he
had welded the cow backwards, with its rear end to
the wind instead of facing it. "That's a fine job you
did," I told him, not wanting to point out his mistake.
"It's a funny thing," he later told me, "but most
regular weathervanes show the cow facing the wind.
Any clod knows a cow never does that."

At the time I wasn't sure about his reasoning, but
later I learned that grazing animals always face away
from the wind. Fliers take particular notice of this
when they want to ascertain wind direction.

My farmer friend is dead now and when they tore
the barn down, I got my cow back. She won't point
out the wind any more but she does much more. She
brings back the memory of a good friend and his
New England logic which I salute with a chuckle and
a good wish wherever his winds are blowing.

way in reducing buildings to a state of "pleasing decay," the effect can reach a rare height of artistic fascination. This is, however, a complex matter because not all ruin is pleasing. Life too mirrors Nature. Man's life passes away all too quickly, and even the best memory is, in some way, a ruin.

There is no building that does not develop some unexpected charm with age; but the early American barn, taking into consideration its reasons for being, I've found to be an exceptional and impressive subject. The growth of moss, the dust of old hay, the powdering of mortar in joints, the mellowing of cut stone, the aging of wood—all things usually thought to be unfortunate—are really Nature's triumph and worth regarding with some (at least artistic) respect. When eyes are opened to pleasing decay, it is sometimes difficult to focus on anything else. Ancient homes have a way of adapting to the changing times; with new curtains and a coat of paint, the appealing quality of age vanishes all to soon, but an old barn has an aura of persistence, stubbornly shrouded in the mood of its own time.

Old farm buildings are monuments to a dead and vanished America. The United States was founded on agrarianism, and the farm was the living symbol of our economy, but that national philosophy has now become obsolete. Replaced by capitalism, the old-time farmer is vanished Americana along with the agrarian credo. Nonetheless, its truth and logic, its reverence for the earth and the God who created it, make it an everlasting religion. Perhaps after capitalism has expended itself (as some logicians predict), man may spend his last efforts on earth in an attempt to return to agrarianism.

After having painted hundreds of pictures of barns and having sketched details of thousands, I have sometimes looked back and wondered if I could have been mistaken to do so. I so passionately believe in the merits of agrarianism that I could have been carried away by nostalgic emotion. Perhaps the magic of my subject had only been an illusion? Yet the incense of hay and animal odors do seem to linger even after a century or two; the sense of harbor from the outside world given by an old barn does prevail like a persistent ghost. To me a barn's age has actual dimension and proportion; even after it has fallen and its timbers disappeared, there seems to be some part of it lingering, looming above the stone foundations. All this may sound absurd: I am simply stating what I feel.

Historically speaking, barns have usually been overlooked, although they speak more truthfully of the past than most architectural monuments. Their sameness of construction in America is often regarded as a lack of originality, or perhaps an indication of the early Puritan starvation of self-expression. Actually their sameness represents nothing other than a reverence for tradition. The farmer of the past had much more building education and appreciation of art than today's farmer, yet there was no urge for self-expression or for "change for the sake of change." From Maine to Virginia (though nationalities and personalities differed), you will find beams cut in the very same manner and fastened together into designs almost as if they had all been done by the same person.

In the study of barn architecture, you come closer to pure Americana than in old homes in which European and English influences all but eliminated any standard American style. Both in research that proved useful and for pure personal pleasure, I think I've done well to have remembered barns.

Wisconsin Swedish
c. 1860

GAMBREL

Pennsylvania German 1790

FORE BAY

57

The subject of some hundred illustrations and some magazine covers, this old barn was one of my first recollections of Bucks County, Pennsylvania. I came upon it late on a winter afternoon with the setting sun lighting the red-painted boards of its banked overhang. I find that sunlight not only brightens but changes the color of whatever it highlights; therefore the true color of anything is best seen within shade. Certainly the sunlit red-painted wood was not so brilliant and orange-tinted; the true color is seen in the shadowed portions.

So-called hex signs are nothing but a farmer's self-expression and an attempt to decorate a building he was proud of. His wife used the same sort of stars and circles when she created a patchwork blanket. I find the frequent references to the American farmer's hex lore unfounded and misleading comments about a religious and logical person.

...there were great Stone Barns

Pennsylvania
1779

FEW BUILDINGS OF THE PAST REMAIN TO SPEAK AS plainly of the early American economy as the old stone farm buildings. Everything the New World meant to the first German farmers of Pennsylvania seems to be expressed in these monumental structures.

European farmers were not lords of the land, as were the farmers in pioneer America. They did not own large farm buildings; the sheds for sheltering a horse or two and for storing a few farm implements were not even regarded as true barns. The only stone barns in England and Europe were tithe storehouses that belonged to the landlords, the king, or to the church. Only in America could a peasant gather his own stones and erect such a castlelike building. In Europe the farmer usually lived either above or at one end of that part of the building housing his animals, but when he moved to America, his animals

61

A door opening to outside summer is always a framed greeting. This door, a mate to the painting on page xi, was in the same stone barn and was built of horizontal and vertical slabs of virgin pine, "deadened" together with hand-wrought nails.

"Dutch doors" were designed to keep out animals, but the effect of the top half being open and the bottom shut, transforms the door into a window. Like the barns they were attached to, they should be called German rather than Dutch; the man who made this barn and its door, was named Ludwig Weiss; his initials and the date he arrived from Germany— 1746—were carved into the other side.

were housed separately. The New World farmer had a home of his own, apart from his barn. In the days of the American Revolution there were nearly a thousand stone barns in America, some over a hundred feet long; their construction was as strong as possible so that they might last for centuries and be handed down from generation to generation. I doubt if there are any barns being built as well today, or with the thought of passing them on to sons or daughters. The extraordinary family spirit and agrarian economy that originally sparked America are gone; only the old stone barns are left to remind us of it.

Pennsylvania's stone barns were built to copy (or outdo) European tithe barns, but this was not the case in New England, where there is today an almost total absence of stone barns. There, where "stones grow as a main crop," you will find only clap-

New Jersey
1780

65

With the caboose at one side and the farmhouse running completely out of the picture, this is how I remember the place where I worked as a farmhand for fifty cents a day. After one month of beautifully satisfying labor I accidentally let the hay-wagon horses get out of control which resulted in broken reins and torn harness. After paying for the damage, my walkaway salary was a dollar and a half and as many apples as I could take with me.

Most New Hampshire farms were attached or continuous when I was there in 1922, but new insurance laws have made the design impractical, and so a quaint New England building style has all but vanished. In a heavy snowstorm the style has more than quaintness.

board or shingled farmhouses and wooden barns. Although stone fences are a symbol of New England, there are not more than a few stone farm buildings remaining in the area. New Englanders had a reverence for wood, which was further shown by their practice of leaving their houses unpainted so that the wood might season quicker and acquire a patina of its own.

One mystery of the old Pennsylvania stone barns is that their walls have so seldom cracked. Even the best-made house today will "settle" after a short time, yet there are many lofty stone barns built by simple Pennsylvania farmers that have lasted over two centuries without showing any settling cracks. The red sandstone of Berks County, the weathered mica schist of the Philadelphia area, the granites of Lehigh County, and the gray limestone walls of Bucks County were all put together with various individual patterns and "butterings" of pointing cement, but I have yet to see one pulling apart at the seams. Perhaps the "self-healing" qualities of calcified lime mortar had a sealing and weatherproofing quality. Whatever the secret, the farmer-builders of early Pennsylvania were geniuses at working with stone.

The artist who paints rocks and stone walls derives real pleasure from seeing their textures appear on his canvas. When working on solid Masonite, I find that scraping my painted rocks with a razor blade will often produce accidental textures that are better than anything that could be achieved purposely with only the brush. By overpainting and scraping time and time again, remarkable effects are obtained. I guess I've used as many razor blades on my paintings as I've used brushes.

Continuous farm architecture in Europe usually involved a complete square of buildings, forming a barnyard in the center. American continuous architecture started from the farm dwelling with breezeway to summer kitchen, wash-house, and well-pantry, and with other connecting barns strung out and away (usually downhill) like a train of railroad cars. I remember them well, for during my first try as a boy farmhand, I slept in the farthermost lean-to, which the German farmer called the "caboose." (Actually the railroad term "caboose" is derived from the German *cabinaus—cabaus*, or "cabin-house.") There I lived for the whole summer—in New England, where the American connecting barn was born.

Forty years later, I made a professional study of continuous architecture. I found that it began in New Hampshire because of the great snows there, and then the idea spread to eastern Vermont and Maine, down through Massachusetts, and ended with a scattered few through the northern part of Connecticut. The last known example was on the property I bought in Warren, Connecticut: the carriage barn was still connected and intact (it became my living room); unfortunately, the other connected barns had been removed about half a century earlier. I once returned to that New Hampshire farm where I had worked and found it overgrown with grass and weeds, and the barns unused. The shed I'd lived in had been taken over by a family of raccoons.

No more continuous farm architecture is now being built, partly because there is no way to group various outbuildings under one insurance policy. So the connected barn has become part of a vanished America, but the thought of a farmer being able to go from his kitchen to as many as a dozen barns without venturing out into a blizzard still holds fascination. I recall how, during each hard rain, I passed through a haybarn, a milking shed, a pantry-house,

Pennsylvania's style of stone barn construction stops abruptly at the banks of the Delaware. New Jersey farmers had just as much stone, but they usually chose wood. This building (now demolished) was one of the few New Jersey stone barns I have ever seen. Without the overhanging bay of the German "bank" design, Jersey barns were smaller and less pretentious, aesthetically poorer, and were never painted or decorated in any way. I know that many people profess to sense a difference in passing over a state line without knowing exactly what that difference is. Between Pennsylvania and New Jersey one noticeable difference is in the barns.

I recall doing several sketches of this barn and when a late summer squall interrupted, I went inside to escape the downpour. Although the roof was worn and broken to the extent that I could easily see the sky through it, not a drop of rain came through when the storm arrived: the soft cedar shingles padded with moss had closed quickly with the oncoming low pressure of the storm.

and a woodshed on my way to breakfast. My trips now from my bedroom to my kitchen are definitely less fascinating.

Another vanished example of national architecture is the American round barn. While researching, I found only three of them left in Pennsylvania, over a dozen in Vermont, and about two hundred scattered throughout the West. Nebraska had over two dozen.

Perhaps the best-known round barn is the stone example at Hancock Shaker Village Museum in Massachusetts. My painting of this is reproduced in my book *An Age of Barns,* and I tell how the barn was originally designed to house fifty-two cows. Josiah K. Lilly, III, who while creating his famous Heritage Plantation at Sandwich, Massachusetts, needed a proper building for displaying a collection of fifty-two early automobiles, came across my Shaker round-barn story and decided he had found the answer. Because automobiles are a bit longer than cows, however, Mr. Lilly added another ten feet to his building; except for that, he constructed an exact replica of the Hancock Shaker barn. I feel this alone made my book a worthwhile project, for now there are *two* great round stone barns in Massachusetts, both beautifully preserved for posterity.

The round barn and the continuous-architecture barn are members of those few and rare items completely American. Nobody is entirely sure how the early round barn evolved; in my writing I have commented that "inasmuch as cows are not pie-shaped, I can't imagine why a barn should be round." But the University of Illinois gave me battle. "Sloane is wrong," they said. "Cows certainly *are* pie-shaped and their movements within their stalls are definitely triangular. So even in rectangular barns, stalls should be pie-shaped." Researchers, I've learned, should never make personal comments—just state the facts.

During a more recent period of doing paintings of barn interiors, I decided I had found a new magic; and after spending a few days within the quiet, hypnotic confines of an ancient barn, I knew the magic was real. Wordsworth said, "Thou whose exterior semblance doth belie thy soul's inner immensity," and this expresses exactly what I felt, for from the outside you view ruins, but from within you seem to be in actual contact with an immense living past. So I ended my work of depicting barn exteriors and I began a time of painting interiors.

Windows are the constant eyes of a house, staring without emotion; a door has many moods. The open door is like an invitation. It tempts you to explore within; from the inside it frames enticement to the bright outside world. When a door is left ajar, there is a baffling fascination of uncertainty about what is happening within or without. The ruin of an old barn whose door has fallen off has always been a special invitation to me, particularly when both doors of the threshing bay have gone and the dark interior frames a distant landscape beyond. I suspect a painter might spend his life depicting only doorway scenes, with the certainty that each beholder would accept the painter's request to feel the mood of his work.

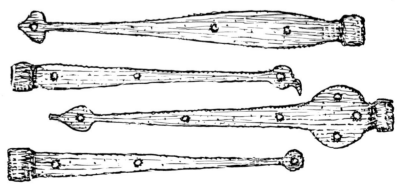

There is a certain time of day when the sun is low, the shadows become deeper, the light becomes brighter, and the distant hills loom "nearer." This old barn riding on a sea of ripened grass, a Dutch structure with oversized roof, reflected the waning sunlight and offered itself as a subject, symbolic of a thousand recollections.

THIS RUIN WAS MY FIRST BARN. ONLY A SMALL CON-
necticut horse-and-wagon barn, it had been deserted for about a century and was too far gone to
repair. I ordered its removal, but I saved all of its
hand hewn beams for my studio ceiling.

A local farmer accepted the work of dismantling
it, and shortly after our agreement, as I lay in bed
one night thinking sentimentally about the old structure, there was a loud crash. The farmer, I mused,
had been deprived of his demolition job by the rav-
ages of time. But when I took a lantern uphill to see
what had happened, I found him hard at work without any other light than the moon. I had never seen
anyone work in the dark before, but he assured me
everything was under control and that he could see
very well. I learned that he, like the early farmers
did many of his summer odd jobs after dark.

The incident explained to me why the old al-
manacs contained so much moon-phase information.
I had regarded this as superstition, but a little research unearthed the fact that roofing, haying, drov-
ing, and many other summertime farm chores were
best done during the cool of night and by the light
of the moon. And I did come to the conclusion that
the early American had much better eyesight (certainly better night-sight) than we have today.

This barn probably inspired me to do my first
book on the subject. When the building was leveled
and I had begun pulling the plastered foundation
masonry apart, I found the imprint of the builder's
hand. Every line, callous, and scar was there, and as
I placed my hand into the imprint to compare sizes,
I had the strange feeling of someone from the past
reaching down through the years to touch me. Right
then and there I decided to study and understand
that early American, the Barn Builder.

This is the round barn at Hancock, Massachusetts. The silo at the left is not as old as the round stone barn structure, although the barn, built in 1826, was itself really a sort of combination barn and silo. Some antiquarians will be surprised to learn that the well-known wooden silo did not come into being until the twentieth century.

The replica at Sandwich

Not long ago a man with fifty-two very mint antique automobiles had been trying to decide what kind of building he should build to house his collection for public display. His architect suggested a large New England-type barn. Then one night as he was dozing off to sleep while reading my book An Age of Barns he saw the plan of the Shaker round stone barn "for fifty-two cows." Misreading the copy, he suddenly became wide awake. But what is good for fifty-two cows, he thought, might also be good for

fifty-two cars! I have solved my problem!

And so Josiah K. Lilly III went about building an exact copy of the Shaker barn at Hancock on his famous restoration "Heritage Plantation" in Sandwich, Massachusetts. Cars are a bit longer than cows so about ten feet was added to the diameter of the replica; otherwise stone for stone and beam for beam you may today see a perfect copy of the great old building, as utilitarian a design as when it was first thought of in 1826.

Vermont

Although the round barn concept was called a
"noble experiment" a century and a half ago, it is now
considered a symbol of modern architecture. With
about a hundred ancient examples still standing
and in operation, some farmers are building the
"early American" round (and polygonal) barns.

This composition of shapes and angles was what confronted me when I first climbed into the attic of what is now my studio building. The room to the right has become a bedroom. Homes cannot be transformed into barns, but the simplicity of a barn always seems adaptable to all sorts of remodelling.

The odor of seasoned wood and rotted hay permeated the old attic, and although it has now been plastered over and refinished, on a hot summer day the good smells of yesterday seem to seep through. The framing beams still bear the marks of broadaxes that shaped tree trunks from this farmland into square beams, and as I lie in bed, it is a pleasure to see their varied patterns. The wainscoting was of rough boards, some a yard wide, and like the word itself (wain for wagon and cote for house) a wainscoted room has the comforting feeling of a sheltered wagon-house. The floorboards were of oak, the beams of chestnut, the wall-boards of pine: each wood of the world of yesterday had its place in architecture; man had a reverence for trees.

This interior shows a bright morning light breaking into the darkness of the Shaker apple-barn at Hancock, Massachusetts. Once housing a ceiling-high cider press with black walnut wood gears, the barn also had bins for storing corn. The thick stone walls maintained the constant coolness necessary for storing apples and corn, and the south windows were usually closed against the sun. I opened the shutters and found that the light picked up a brilliance in the shiny Indian corn, lending color to an otherwise solemn composition. But the cellarlike feeling persisted.

This was the first barn interior I had painted, and the dark closure of thick walls seemed to bring alive a mood I had often felt but never expressed. It resulted in a whole year of "dark interiors," which delighted me although the word from the art galleries was, "too solemn to be popular as wall decorations." Solemn or not, the gallery misjudged the popular taste, and I am thankful that barn interior paintings still find their way to living room walls.

Covered Bridges are for Remembering

FOR A FEW YEARS CORNWALL BRIDGE, AN ANCIENT covered structure near my farmhouse in Connecticut, stood in the shadow of a new concrete arch over the Housatonic River. Trucks and cars zoomed overhead, and few people noticed the historic bridge below. There were initials carved into its wood, which had been hauled by ox sleds from North Adams, Massachusetts, over a century before; there were posters still clinging to the wood—posters ad-

vertising auctions held during the Civil War; there were, in the dark tunnel of the bridge, the acrid smells of hay and dust and the musty odor of aged wood. I remember with sadness the flood of 1936 and seeing beams and planks, that only an hour before had been Cornwall Bridge, smashed against the concrete stanchions of the new arch.

Few things seem to warm the hearts of antiquarians as much as the ever popular, all-American

Situated on a dirt road and already decaying, this is how I recall the Fairfax Village bridge in Vermont. My original pencil sketch bears its measurements and the documentary information that it was built over Mill Brook in Franklin County. Only as long as my studio living room, the tiny bridge obviously impressed me at the time. If it still stands, I wonder if it would still inspire a painting. Our memory of things is so often greater than the reality.

covered bridge. There are several covered-bridge associations; they publish monthly magazines, hold conventions, and make treks to the thousand or more wooden bridges still standing. Ceremonies, sandwiches, speeches, and note-comparing establish the old bridges as nostalgic meeting places, emblems of the American past.

As a garden ornament, I built a wooden replica of a covered bridge. It is only fifteen feet long, so even a small child has to crawl on his hands and knees to get through it. Yet it is listed and pictured in a covered-bridge directory, and buffs still come from across the nation to photograph it and take measurements.

I'll always remember the sale of my first covered-bridge painting because it really *wasn't* that at all. I'd tried my hand at a few landscapes that featured old Connecticut tobacco barns; they sold quickly, and I wondered why. Quaint as they are, those very long single-story barns have very little architectural beauty. Yet there was a period of research when I did over a dozen sketches of them each week. "People sure must like tobacco barns," I commented to my gallery manager. "Don't say that," he replied sternly. "They think those are covered bridges." Indeed at a distance the long boxlike Connecticut tobacco barn looks exactly like a covered bridge. But a tobacco barn is just a tobacco barn; a covered bridge is a national monument.

Nearly three decades ago, when I decided to paint covered bridges, I thought I might first do some research in order to know my subject better. At that time, as I said earlier, the easiest way for me to learn about anything was to write a book about it— and that is what I did . The book, *American Barns and Covered Bridges,* is still selling (more now than when it first appeared), so it would seem that people have an ever mounting reverence for the old bridges.

Vermont has become known as "the covered-bridge state," and wooden bridges are regarded by most as New England Americana. The truth is that New England has fewer of them than Pennsylvania (first), Ohio (second), Indiana (third), and Oregon (fourth). Vermont is only fifth! I remember sketching sixty covered bridges in Indiana, fifty in Georgia, and thirty-five in Kentucky. In 1950 there were at least fifteen hundred old wooden bridges left (anyhow, I painted or sketched that many). Placed side by side, they would stretch to about half a mile of artwork, so it's understandable that I'm all through with painting covered bridges.

When I was trying to recall the first covered bridge I painted, my recollection resulted in this picture of the Lovejoy bridge over the Ellis River in Maine. Its slanted portal hoods made it look less like "a tobacco barn stretched over a river," and the red paint had nearly weathered away, leaving a mural of textured boards spanning the reflecting water.

I thought it a fine subject for my first try. An old timer passed by with a load of hay but he stopped long enough to give me some of the bridge's history. It had been built in 1866 and the 85-foot span had cost $743.47. I liked that kind of Maine exactness, so when I placed the painting in a gallery for sale, I marked the price at what the bridge itself had cost. But that was a very long while ago, and my gallery manager, not having a sense of humor, objected to the odd price. "Make it an even $750.00," he said gruffly. "That way you know your painting brought more than the damned bridge!"

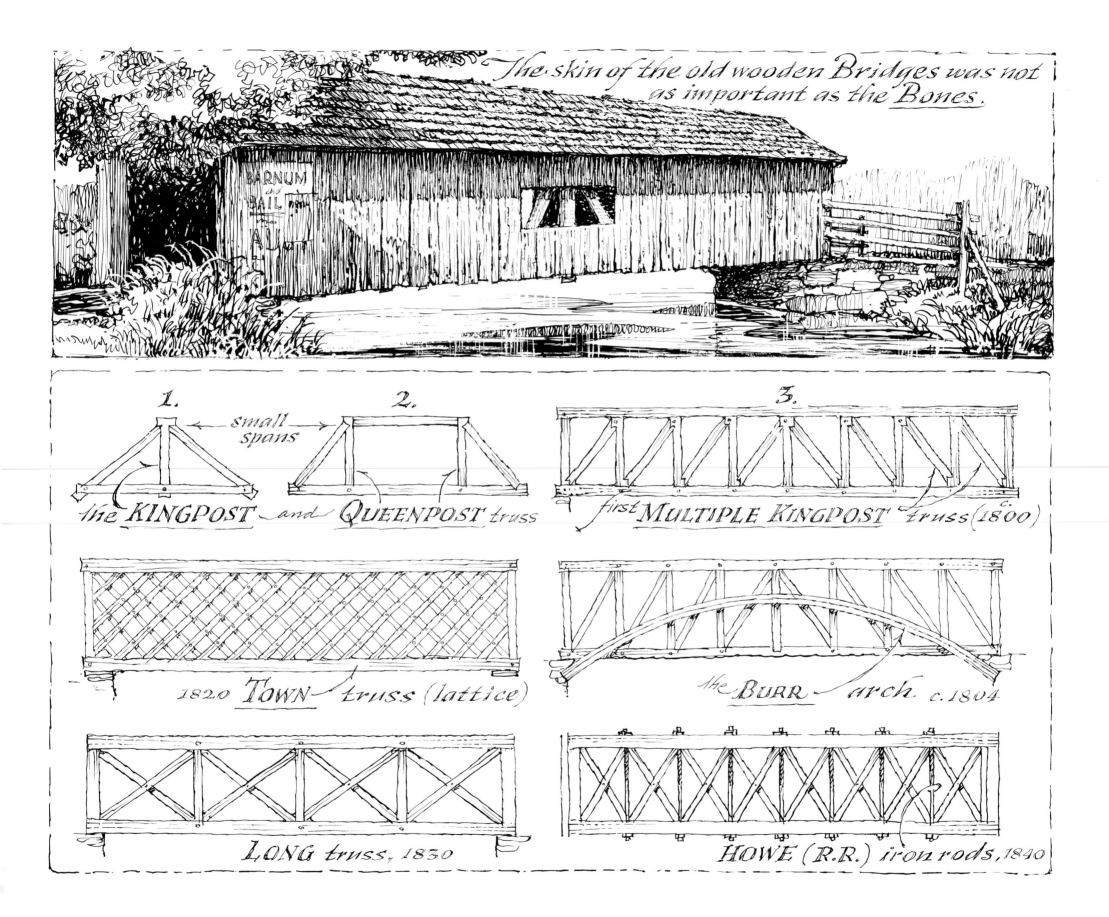

The skin of the old wooden Bridges was not as important as the Bones.

BARNUM and BAIL

1. small spans
the KINGPOST and 2. QUEENPOST truss

3. first MULTIPLE KINGPOST truss (c. 1800)

1820 TOWN truss (lattice)

the BURR arch c.1804

LONG truss, 1830

HOWE (R.R.) iron rods, 1840

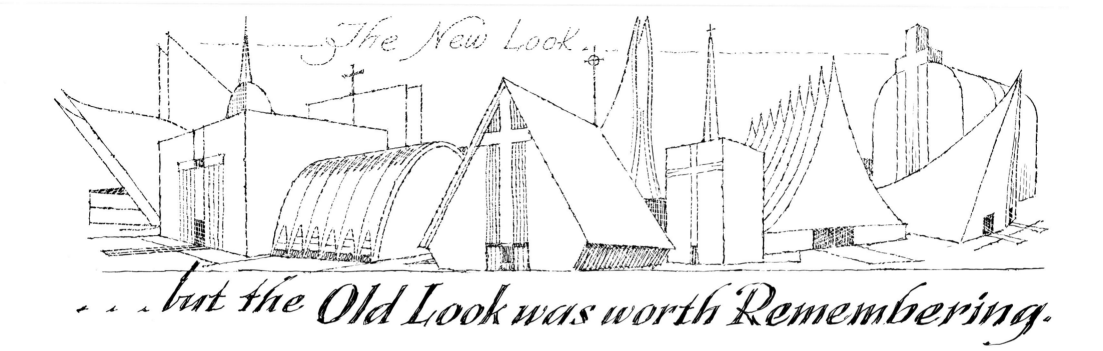

The New Look . . .

. . . but the Old Look was worth Remembering.

AS WITH ALL ART, THE NEW LOOK IN CHURCH ARCHI-tecture is explained as a reflection of the scientific times in which we live. Yet much of modern life and of modern art is pure escapism; it is too often diversion simply for the sake of change. I believe that change can be as bad as it can be good, but religion and acceptance of God should be that part of life with the most permanence, and the architecture of religion ought to reflect this truth.

One book I never finished dealt with early American churches, and was to be illustrated with paintings. I started with some of the ancient churches on the north shore of Long Island. Those were lean years, when selling my work was of first importance, so I contemplated the idea of selling the original paintings to the people who had been married in those churches; it seemed an extraordinarily appro-priate wedding-anniversary gift. But I found that a good many of the people who had been married in the churches I'd chosen to paint were, unfortunately, already divorced. It was evidence of changing times —and no help to my pocketbook!

Doing research for that book, I learned that the first American villages were built around their churches. The town square or village green with its church was always the hub; homes came next, then came a proper scattering of stores and industry. But the church on the green was the real center of the early American community.

Today the worship of money has apparently be-come stronger than the worship of God—the center of each community now is its bank. Even in roadside shopping centers, only when a bank joins the group does the complex become recognized as an established community. I once thought of suggesting that banks cap their buildings with churchlike steeples topped with gold dollar signs where a church usually has a cross, but the idea is really more tragic than funny. Most people are unaware of the height that the worship of money has reached. About fifteen years ago, while I was speaking on this subject before a church group, several in my audience interrupted to declare me wrong—they indeed did *not* worship money. So as I spoke on, I took one dollar bill after another from my pocket and began tearing them into small pieces. The same people were visibly shaken and shocked at such a sight; one even remarked that my act was sacrilegious. It was only a couple of dollars, as much as we waste in some way or another each week, yet when I returned to speak at that church fifteen years later, they remembered me. "My father is dead now," one man said, "but he heard you speak. You're the man who tore up dollar bills."

From where I sit in my studio I can see a church spire rising just above the treeline, in the center of Warren village. At the top of a small hill, this building was erected by ordinary farmers and local carpenters when money was scare and mechanical time-savers unknown; yet its excellence for some reason cannot be duplicated today. The architectural know-how of making beautiful church spires has been lost, and according to modern building practices, to try to revive it would be too expensive (strange reasoning during an age of riches and waste). A few modern churches do sometimes add a tiny steeple, almost as a symbolic afterthought, and the result is pathetic. God is not dead; His architects, however, are certainly declining.

Those steeples pointing to heaven through the countryside have inspired Americans for two centuries, and it seems a pity to see them disappear. Asher Benjamin, one of our few architects of the 1700s, designed a variety of church spires with the conviction that the words "spire" and "inspiration" had a common root. Plato said, "When the poet functions properly, he is inspired," and being inspired is "being breathed into by the god." The words "spiritual" and "inspiring" are aroused in my mind every time I see a spire.

"Tradition has become an ugly word in this age of revolution, and so it has become fashionable to revolt against things traditional. Yet you might as well revolt against understanding and belief and learning and culture; these things are usually the standards of tradition. *Tradition* deserves a second look and some serious study before we cast away something of the greatest value. Christianity itself is traditional." These words were spoken at a recent meeting of architects in discussing the popular trend of "non-traditional church architecture."

Few changes have saddened me more than the new modernistic buildings which have now begun to house the church. They should symbolize Christianity, yet I have seen modern churches that more resemble Carvel stands, cement tents, world's fair concessions, enlarged gas stations, prisons, warehouses, and almost anything but the standard design of the American church. In the parish house of the Old Ship Meeting House at Hingham, Massachusetts, are carved the words, "Let the Work of Our Fathers Stand." Unless we can build something better (not just different), I think there would be more merit in simply reproducing the work of our fathers.

Spires of American

Yesterday

WHENEVER I VISITED A VILLAGE DURING THE WANDER-
ings of my youth, I made a special effort to view the
place from a height; the tallest place in town was
sometimes a hill, but usually it was a church. I remember, as a child, poring through William Cullen
Bryant's twin-volume *Picturesque America* and no-
ticing that the Hudson River School illustrators frequently made their sketches of America's towns as
seen from a church steeple. Those extraordinary
artists chose to climb nearly inaccessible heights and
look down at their subject. Because of the strange
fascination that is given by height, the result was
sometimes nightmarish, but always unforgettable.
Today's painters have either grown lazy or lack
imagination, for most of us modern landscapers seem
to choose to sit comfortably before our subject and
look squarely at it, and the result is usually a post-
card effect.

You can seldom explain likes or dislikes, but I
have always liked church steeples. They are, of
course, oustandingly difficult things to collect. I
knew a man who once bought the tower of a church
that was being demolished, then placed it on a rocky
promontory at his summer seaside place as a gazebo.
If I were rich, I decided, I would do that same thing.

When I first moved to northern Connecticut, the
old Warren Congregational Church steeple lay resting on the ground while a new one was being hoisted
into place. I made an immediate and rash offer for
the old steeple (without knowing exactly what I'd
do with it except save it from the town dump), and
my offer was quickly accepted. So I owned a church
steeple even before I owned my house in Warren.
But although I found no proper place for my steeple
(and it finally *did* end in the dump), I pursued another personal antiquarian interest. To the satisfac-

This church painting was done a long while ago, from a sketch made while scouting the hills of New Hampshire in a Model T Ford. Like a house attached to a tower, many old New England churches had a sizeable entrance room for the hats and coats and blankets and boots and the foot-warming equipment needed for old-time New England churchgoing. The entrance room of this church even had its own window.

Contrary to the rule of most New England country churches, this one faced west, but the cemetery tombstones faced east and the rising sun—awaiting reincarnation, according to legend.

When painting the sky, I am often asked, "Is this a sunset or a sunrise scene?" The best way to tell is that cumulus, or lumpy, clouds occur in the afternoon, while a cloudless or stratus filled sky is indicative of morning. This painting shows the disintegration of storm clouds at the end of the day, with the setting sun shining upon them from the west.

Nothing pierces a cloudscape with more dignity or meaning than the spire of an old church. The first spire of the Warren church once looked like this, but the only original part left now is the weathervane, which has a fish-tail and arrow design. A half-ton bell swings on a wagon-type wheel; mechanized now, the wheel used to be turned by a rope that hung down the spire and into the choir balcony below. Struck by lightning and changed a few times by remodeling, the new spire has become "New England wedding cake" in design, staccato with frills and decoration; but it still looks to me like one of the beautiful churches in the country.

tion of the elders of the church, I offered to install a clock for their church's ancient church bell. I've always liked bells too—I even wrote a book about them.

When the mechanized Warren church bell sounds throughout the night now, it lulls me to satisfied content: it is soft and comforting—and a mile away. But I suppose (and worry too) that there are neighbors closer to the bell who may be less satisfied with its hourly clanging.

Although church bells were an important part of early America, they didn't just count the hours. They announced the beginning of the day's work at six, the mealtime at noon, the end of day at nine. They announced the start and end of town meetings, church assemblies, the arrival of news (before newspapers); and there was a code for many civic alarms. They announced each death in town, even telling the sex of the deceased (six tolls for a woman and nine for a man), and then they knelled the actual age by a muted stroke each minute, one for each year.

One most interesting thing I discovered was that ringing bells on Independence Day was an early American custom. I also found that the practice was changed during the Civil War, when guns and fireworks took over the celebration. But bells, to me, typify freedom more than the sounds of war do, and I thought bell-ringing might be a good custom to revive. And so one day in 1962, as I sat talking about this with my author-neighbor Eric Hatch, I decided to do something about it.

By 1963 a Congressional resolution was passed, asking that all public bells be rung at 2 P.M. (E.D.T.) on July Fourth. Governor Dempsey of Connecticut was the first of all the Governors to include this request in his annual Independence Day Proclamation. My wife set up an office in a spare bedroom and sent out newsletters to fifty thousand churches and to thousands of mayors and selectmen; within five years the idea was established as the revival of an early American custom. If it continues in America, I'm sure I can consider this one of the most important accomplishments of my life. It seems to me disgraceful that many of our holidays, such as Christmas or Easter, have deteriorated into nothing but gala shopping sprees; perhaps the church bells can at least help keep our nation's birthday meaningful.

A part of my project of ringing bells on Independence Day was to get handbells to the American Indian children in New Mexico, where I once lived. Surely the Indians should have part in the celebration, I thought, so one day I set out for the Southwest with a truckload of handbells. Shortly after my arrival in Taos, I persuaded the Indian Governor of that Pueblo to officiate, and he gave each child a bell. Santa Fe and surrounding villages liked the idea too, and hundreds of ancient bells (some hidden away for many years) were readied for ringing on that July Fourth. Strangely enough, some of the oldest bells in all of America came to light, many brought from Europe during the 1600s to be used in the earliest Mexican missions.

One day a very old Indian came to me with the gift of a bell. "This," he said in Spanish, "was from an old ship wrecked more than two hundred years ago on the Atlantic coast. There is also a letter that tells about it."

It wasn't really a letter, but rather a short history of the bell. It was written on crumbling rag paper and it told how the bell was from a British merchant ship built in 1732. "Her last voyage," it read, "delivered a bell to Isaac Norris of Philadelphia to be used in the jubilee of the 1701 Charter." That bell didn't reach Philadelphia in time, according to history, and when it did arrive, it cracked. It was recast, but it cracked again. It was recast a second time and finally was hung in the State House at Philadelphia. There it rang like any other bell in America until July 4, 1776. On that day it pealed to celebrate the adoption of the Declaration of Independence, and from that day on it has been known as the Liberty Bell.

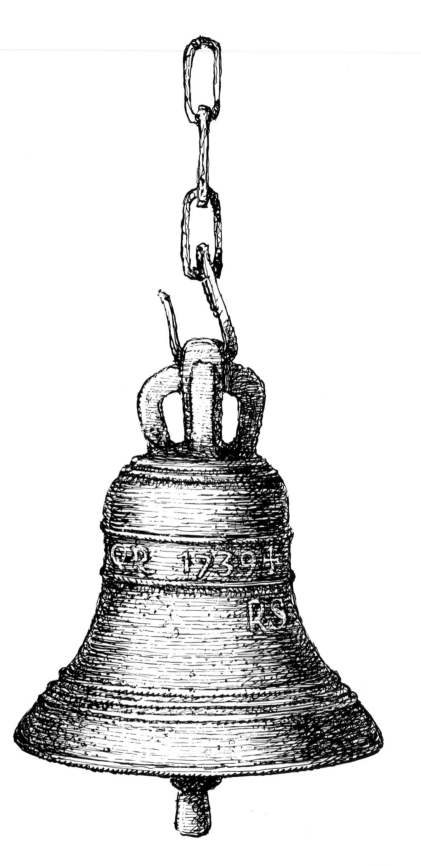

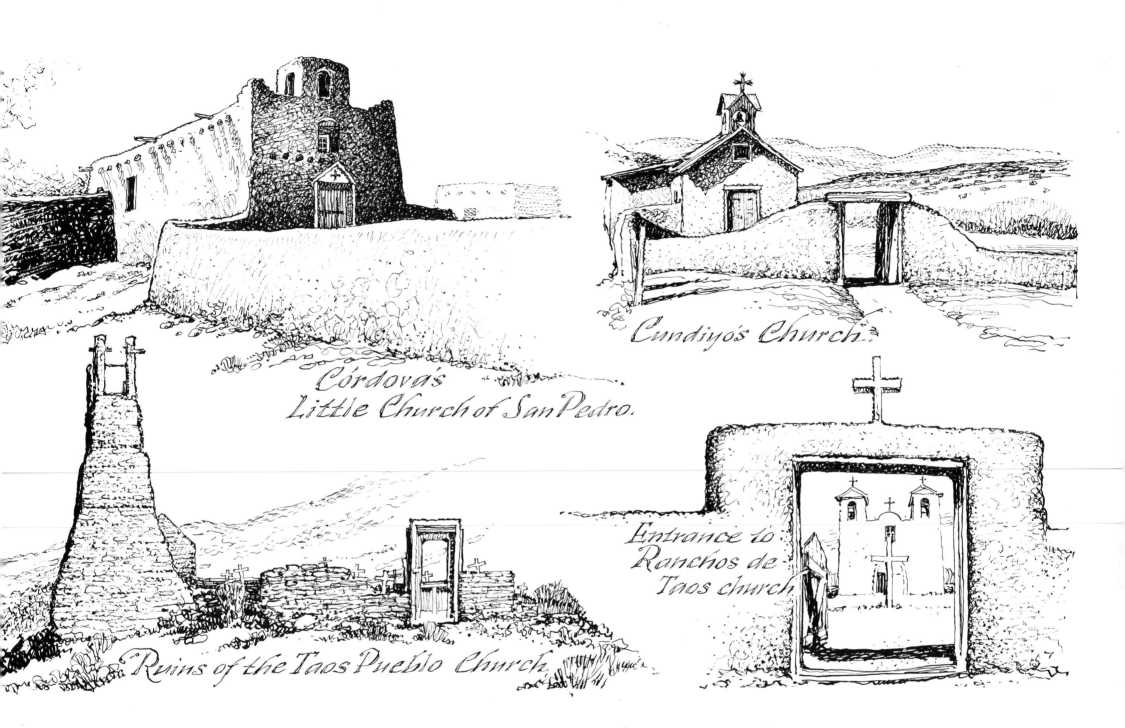

Córdova's
Little Church of San Pedro.

Cundiyo's Church.

Ruins of the Taos Pueblo Church

Entrance to
Ranchos de
Taos church

IT SEEMS STRANGE THAT THE OLDEST CHURCHES IN America were made of only common mud and straw. I remember using my knapsack sign-painting kit, nearly half a century ago, in portrayals of the ancient Taos pueblo church ruins: there in New Mexico this and other churches stood long before the Pilgrims arrived at Plymouth, Massachusetts. I recall how the adobe arms of the ruined belfry tower were raised as in a sign of truce, just as were the arms of the Indian rebels who once sought refuge there. Our troops nevertheless cannoned the church and killed its occupants, thus establishing it as an historic and mean-

front view,
St. Francis
of Assisi --
Taos.

ingful monument. An ancient weather-beaten door opened into a roofless outdoor room, which was floored with dozens of wooden crosses where the murdered Indians were buried so long ago.

There are still scores of adobe churches thereabouts, gems of Southwestern architecture that are defying the encroaching junk age. The Ranchos de Taos church (St. Francis Mission) is still a "symphony in mud" with walls nearly six-feet thick. Soft-drink signs, tourist debris, and an outdoor movie now despoil the sanctity of the neighborhood, yet the profound dignity of early days is fairly indestructible. I remember watching the people of Ranchos de Taos giving their church a periodic plastering. Mud was mixed by the feet of the men, and then carried by children to the women, who did the actual plastering high up on pine-pole scaffolds. The painting on page 107 (done after such a plastering project long ago) reflects the intense coloring of the New Mexican sunset. This shows the back of the church (built in the shape of a cross), and unlike the inviting courtyard of its entrance (page 105), it offers on uncluttered bulwark of abstract shapes set protectingly against the highway only a few yards away. Inside is a painting of Christ walking on the shores of Galilee; in complete darkness the portrait becomes luminous and the shadow of a cross being carried by the figure becomes visible. People still come to gaze in wonder at this phenomenon.

I suppose the adobe churches of the Southwest might remain intact for another century or so, although the reverence for tradition wanes with the increasing momentum of life today. The ornateness of typical Spanish church architecture matched the sometimes cruel complexity of early Catholicism, but the plainness of the Indian country mission spoke only of holy simplicity. There was a carved wooden board in the Taos church that said, "Simplicity and holiness becomes Thy house, O Lord."

Amen to that.

Painted in a technique different from the one I use today, this picture was done while I lived in Taos. It expresses astonishment at the colors of the Indian country, more than the nostalgic mood which characterizes my paintings of today.

The planes of adobe sunlight and shadow change constantly, but the solidness of the old St. Francis of Assisi mission at Ranchos de Taos remains as it was in 1718. Known as the "symphony in mud," its simplicity and feeling of shelter suggest to me its true reason for being as few other churches do.

Lo, the poor Indian.

IN MANY MORE WAYS THAN THE BASIC MEANING THAT the word indicates, Tony Luhan was a *big* man. Even when he came to New York every few years with his wife, Mabel Dodge, he followed the Taos Indians' tribal custom of wearing a bedsheet. Once when he stayed with me for a visit, he purchased a large quantity of huge sheets from Lord & Taylor. Then, one night at the Number One Bar on Fifth Avenue, we *both* wore sheets, and with the help of some firewater to make him talk more than he ordinarily did, we had quite a chat. "Really, Tony," I asked him, "what do you fellows think of the white man and how he has taken away your land?"

"You can't *take* land away," he replied solemnly. "The land is always there; one can only borrow it. But you white men have certainly messed it up. That is what we don't like."

I remember the American adobe country as few others do: I have a copy of *Nation's Heritage*, published in 1949, with a picture of a Taos Indian doing the hoop dance. "During this dance which may have begun ten centuries ago," reads the caption, "the

Taos Indian becomes one with his people and one with the gods of the desert." The hoop dance is not quite that old because I originated it! I had made a little wooden hoop for the three-year-old nephew of Juanito Luhan (leader of my Taos dance group), and the child chose to dance with it rather than roll it along the ground. Juanito liked what his tiny nephew did, made a bigger hoop, and began what is now known as "the Taos hoop dance."

I remember Taos without electric lights, without tourists, and with only a few painters. Artists Couse, Sharp, Ufer, Blumenschein, Higgins, Phillips, and Berninghaus had just become the legendary seven of the West and Taos already showed promise of turning into a national bohemia. I recall a special court held late one night in the old Kit Carson house (now a museum) to try a man accused of rape. The penalty at the time was hanging. That lamp-lit scene

Adobe weathers beautifully and becomes wrinkled like the face of an old Indian. Here and there, after a long while, the cracks widen and tiny tufts of straw pop out like the stubble of a beard.

This scene is within the Taos pueblo and was done from a 1926 sketch. At that time, and as far back as the 1850's, all Taos Indians wore a white sheet, either wound into a beltlike sash worn about the waist, or opened and draped over the head as a hood and shawl. Approaching the doorway is the white-sheeted figure of Trinidad, one of a group of Indian dancers I managed at the time.

The western scene is nearly always one of intense light and deeply contrasting shadow. This sketch (one of the first I did on Masonite) was the earliest of a series of shadow-patterned doorways.

Pueblo Church

of white-shrouded Indians and Mexican-shawled women is one I've never forgotten. Taos was once probably the most colorful spot in the United States.

My arrival at Taos was with a disheartened and drunken lumber salesman from Denver whose truck had broken down in Cimarron Canyon. As pay-ment for my help, and because the lettering on my Model-T announced that I painted signs, he gave me his complete supply of "new building-board sam-ples" called Masonite. "They'll never sell anyway," he said. "They're much too hard. But perhaps you can make signs on them."

Later I gave some of my sample Masonite boards to the Taos painters. Leon Gaspard, in whose house I stayed, declared they would be ideal stuff for artists to paint on. He was indeed right, for he and a few of the famous seven tried out the boards and they all liked them. Today more than half of all paintings in the United States are done on Masonite.

Masonite does not tear or shrink as canvas does, and if treated correctly, will last longer. I use it also because I trim or "crop" my work exactly the way a photographer does; sometimes I saw away most of the painting to get a desired effect. Once I sawed a painting in half and sold each piece in a different gallery! Another time a jury member returned a painting for a show because it exceeded the size allowed in the show. "What did you say the limit is?" I asked. "And do have a cup of coffee." Then I took the painting from its frame, sawed it down to size, replaced it into a smaller frame and noticed that amazement had kept the jury member from thinking about his coffee. I'd guess that the saw job might have even added to the painting's quality, for it won the gold medal and went to Europe as "an example of American art." My discovery of Masonite in Taos has continued to pay off.

In going back to New Mexico to write *Return to Taos* (1959), I felt very old and very saddened. The Taos Indians had resisted cement roads and electricity and the pueblo was still one of the few ancient adobe monuments without TV antennas, but the pollution of American "civilization" had already infected the scene. Today, the dignity of old Taos is all but gone. If you ask a Taos Indian what the name "Taos" means, he will look far away as if trying to remember. "At one time," he will finally tell you, "it meant 'the way' or 'the road.'" The way of America has changed now and its roads lead to everywhere and nowhere. On my last visit, I picked up a longhaired hitchhiker and his barefooted wife. Both wore feathers and blankets, mimicking what they presumed to be Indian costume. "We live in Taos," they told me. "It's the greatest. Hasn't changed in centuries."

My interest in doors began, naturally enough, in the adobe country, for there doorways seem to have a special significance. They are even religious symbols, and I have seen several doorways across the top of which was written in Spanish this Biblical quotation: "I am the door; by me if any man enter in, he shall be saved" (John X:9). A Mexican may wear a suit of rags, yet he will sport a fine sombrero; likewise his house may be poor, but it will have a magnificent door. Church enclosures and courtyards will have walls low enough to hurdle over, yet they are entered through impressive doorways. Mable Dodge Luhan of Taos hired an Indian by the year just to carve the doors of her house. The Southwest is indeed a land of interesting and exciting doorways.

In New England, too, the door was more than a closure; the bottom panel often had carved in it a representation of an open Bible, and the top panel a cross. There were "witch" doors to guard against evil entry, white doors to indicate Puritanism, gray doors for the Shakers, and blue doors for the Amish.

Not until I wrote the above did I realize how much doors fascinate me. Now, as I look about my place, I see that as well as many paintings that include doors in their subject matter, I have also hung some ancient doors to decorate the walls, and I have several tables made of old doors(some with hinges intact). When the early American sold his house, he usually took its door with him—so precious was the door to him.

... and *Privies* ...

Delaware

THERE WAS, LONG AGO, A BACKYARD PRIVY AT MY family's country place that had curtains at the window and potted plants on the window sill. We called it the "outhouse," and it was mentioned only when necessary. The ladies called it "the twilight," and I guess that was a prudish (humorous?) twist of the word "toilet." Where I live now certain New Englanders still call it "the nessy" because a century ago privies were referred to as "necessaries." The one I tore down when I remodeled an old farmstead had three holes, and the smallest (for children) was equipped with a tiny platform. It was with some reluctance that I demolished it.

On March 25, 1926, as I went through Kansas with the sign-painter's kit on my back, a very strange thing happened. A farmer returned to his farm and found it had disappeared. Instead there was a thousand-foot hole; the only thing left was a privy, standing on the perimeter of the mysterious volcanolike cavity. I remember this because the farmer turned the little outhouse into an office and sold tickets to all those wishing to view the phenomenon. And it was I who lettered "25 cents admission" on its three walls. This has somewhat substantiated my insistence that I really started my artistic career at the very bottom.

In those days amusing outhouse anecdotes

The Leanto

The Saltbox

The Overbrook

abounded. And if some old-timer were asked to make a list of all the outdated things that could well be forgotten, I guess the outdoor privy might head his whole list. Nevertheless I think of it with some regard, and indeed there are a thousand popular items of modern life I deem more worthy of being forgotten. But "convenience" has become the basic standard of living nowadays, and bringing this particular necessity indoors was one of the outstanding wonders of American science. Great-Grandfather probably doubted the wisdom of placing the "necessary" so centrally, rather than at a polite distance from the living quarters. Even my dog, who is a beast of some sensitivity with an elementary appreciation of privacy, regards me as not being completely housebroken, and he deplores the fact that I sometimes invade his favorite, flushable drinking fountain.

I'll never forget the farmer who helped me remodel my first country place and what he had to say when I started to build an outdoor dining porch. "People used to eat inside," he remarked, "and go to the bathroom outside; now they've switched." Though I accept the disappearance of that private little building without too much longing, I still con-

sider it properly included among subjects of Americana.

Many of the great estates of the 1700s and 1800s had privies to match the architectural design of the manor house. Even small New England estates had privies with vaulted ceilings, fine hinges, and carved moldings. I have found insulated walls in them, while the homestead itself had none. The placing of privies according to privacy and wind direction, and the planting nearby of honeysuckle, wisteria, and lilacs—all that is lost lore. The well-known crescent jigsawed through the door, which originally indicated "Luna" or "femininity," was America's first "ladies' room" sign.

These are obsolete things and probably should be forgotten, yet even the most sophisticated toilet today does what Great-Grandfather would have had more decency and thoughtfulness than to permit. Today it empties directly into the very river that eventually will become the family's drinking water. The thousand or so tons of raw sewage that empty into the Hudson River each hour will some day be purified for New Yorkers. I'm glad I lived in an age that permits me to remember drinking my own spring water.

Privy, necessary house, outhouse, or whatever you wish to call it, this little structure, as far as I know, has been neglected in architectural art.

I have done enough outhouse pictures to compile a sketchbook of "Outhouses I Have Known," and, recalling the success of Chic Sale's "The Specialist," I am sure it would now sell nicely in this unashamed age. But the oldtime privy had a dignity of its own. Small boys were known to turn privies over on Halloween, but they had not yet been encouraged in obscenity, and I have never seen four-letter graffiti on the walls of an old privy. The only examples of wall decoration I came across were a framed sampler with the sewn message of "God Bless This House" and another appropriate sampler quotation from Shakespeare: "For this relief, much thanks; 'tis bitter cold."

The glass-balled lightning rods on the barn in the background, remind me of one privy I came across in Vermont which was equipped with its individual lightning rod.

The Woodshed and the Wheelbarrow

1971

1915

THERE WAS A TIME WHEN SLEDS HAD NAMES. SOME-times the manufacturer stenciled on them fancy titles like the famous *Rosebud* or *Storm King* or *Ice Queen.* Wheelbarrows came with names too—not like the names I've called those ridiculously small-wheeled, metal, modern barrows that sink into the slightest hole and throw you into the air, but nice names such as *Samson* or *Farmer's Helper.* If a young fellow took a particular liking to his wheelbarrow, he painted his best girl's name on it. It may be difficult nowadays to imagine a sane young man taking a liking to a wheelbarrow, but don't forget that I'm referring to a time when people enjoyed doing physical work. Splitting firewood was considered fun for children, and stacking it up was even jollier. And a wheelbarrow was considered quite a birthday or Christmas gift for any young man.

I remember my first wheelbarrow; I named it

Tarzan. I'd just seen the original (silent) screen version of that tale, with Elmo Lincoln playing the title role. He was greater than any man I'd yet seen, and those were the days when children had heroes that looked like strong he-men instead of fops. *Tarzan* was a big wooden wheelbarrow from Sears Roebuck, and it cost two dollars and ten cents. Though faded from nearly half a century of weather, it outlasted a dozen modern, metal barrows. I shall now retire it in the Sloane-Stanley Museum of Early American Tools at Kent, Connecticut. An even older barrow from Montgomery Ward, listed at a dollar and fifty cents in 1898, will take its place in my woodshed. Both the shed and that wheelbarrow are shown in the painting on page 125.

The woodshed I knew as a boy was a wondrous castle of childhood in all seasons. It was a place to ponder worldly things on a rainy day. Splitting wood and arranging it was stimulating to a racing, searching mind while the rain on the roof played an encouraging theme. The shed was a magnificent temple with seasoning wood for incense. There was a wheelbarrow full of hay for use as a couch, and sometimes there were cigarettes and a bottle of ginger brandy. There was always a book or two hidden near the rafters.

How pleasurable are my memories of apple-picking time! The curved-body wheelbarrow was lined with hay and soft gloves were used, both measures being taken to avoid bruising the fruit. That was when the care of apples was still a fine art, and special eating apples were hung by their stems in a cool cellar and would keep for a whole year. There were in those days hundreds of well-known types of apples, and each orchard had its own specialties; today there are only a few types and they are grown for their lasting characteristics rather than for their flavor. Nowadays the whole business of successful agriculture involves storage and sales, rather than quality and taste.

As silly as it may sound, I might quite properly say, "I remember apples." I remember when apple butter was as common as any other butter (I haven't had apple butter for years). Even simple baked apples, once a popular national dessert, have practically vanished from the American menu because it is easier to serve ice cream or fix instant desserts.

The old Carter Farm, when I bought it, had an orchard of ancient apple trees. Other trees in a similar condition would have died years ago; yet broken and nearly barkless, every apple tree still blossoms and bears fruit—fruit that has been feeding the local deer for nearly a century. Tree surgeons suggested I remove the old trees, but I found them even more beautiful than younger trees, so I had them pruned and fed instead. And as if in gratitude, they have given me an extraordinary harvest, as well as offering me subjects for many autumns of painting.

This is a picture showing how my woodshed appeared when I bought the old Carter Farm at Warren. It had been known as "the pig house," and as I began cleaning it to start rebuilding it into a small writing studio, I found evidence of it having been a slaughtering shed during the mid-1700's. I have seen farm slaughtering which long ago ended my fondness for pork dishes.

There has always been something human about pigs (their eyes are closest to ours, and pigskin resembles our skin), and I once bought four pigs for no other reason than to keep them from reaching a butcher. I found them fine pets, and, if fed something other than garbage, they smell no worse than some humans.

The end of the pig house story is that after spending some money to make it a liveable studio, I found that strangely I could produce nothing within its confines. I slept there one night and my nightmares were nearly unbearable. At any rate, my writing studio now makes the most elegant woodshed in the vicinity.

DELIVERING ICE TO THE SUMMER VACATIONISTS WAS my idea of fun during my teens. But the ice business at the lake began to end for the season on Labor Day, and, as the nights grew colder, the Model-T became harder to start in the mornings. The crank case oil hardened each night, and it took all my fifteen-year-old might to crank the pistons through that gummy substance fast enough to get the engine going. The job was simpler, however, if you jacked up the rear wheels, left the engine in gear, and then cranked the whole affair, wheels and all. When you jacked up the rear wheels of a Model-T, you also had a powerful sawmill, for a ten-foot belt around one of the wheels could drive a full-sized circular sawblade. So when the summer ice business ended, the car and I made a fair income by sawing logs into firewood. And that was how I managed to see the inside of so many woodsheds.

As late as 1900 there were many one-room schoolhouses where the accepted "tuition" per pupil was still half a cord of wood; so the school woodshed was often as large or larger than the schoolhouse.

Other than that, I suppose, there never was a set plan or design for the American woodshed; instead, it just seemed to happen. In northern New England the woodshed was attached to the house and the neatly stacked wood inside became part of the overall farm architecture. I've seen several wills in which the wood supply was considered as important an inheritance as any other item.

Trees were the original wealth of the country, and the fascination of working with wood was an American heritage. Chopping firewood or watching a log sever on both sides of a howling blade, then stacking the chunks in piles—these were youthful satisfactions that few young people can comprehend nowadays. Small boys sold *The Saturday Evening Post* and *Youth's Companion* to earn hatchets that clipped to the trouser-belt; mine, called the Dandy Axe, had a leather case, and, except for Sunday, it was part of my daily costume.

Even now the smell of freshly cut wood excites me, and the woodshed memories are a rich pleasure for me.

127

Outside my window is a favorite apple tree. Its main limb was snapped off some three decades ago and someone sawed it flush to the trunk. Most of its bark now serves only as a refuge against the winter for a great variety of living things, and that is good. Still, each autumn this derelict of a tree delivers to me enough fruit for a few pies and apple butter. The apples are pitty and gnarled and not what one might find on a grocer's stand, but they mean something more than just food to me. They also bring deer within close range of my window.

My old Montgomery Ward wheelbarrow, which stood beneath the tree during a fall storm, collected a few dozen fallen apples and created what seemed to be the final touch to a thoughtful symphony of rural subjects. The tree cannot last many more winters; perhaps neither can I or my wheelbarrow. So this painting will have served a purpose, just as have the apple tree and the wheelbarrow and I.

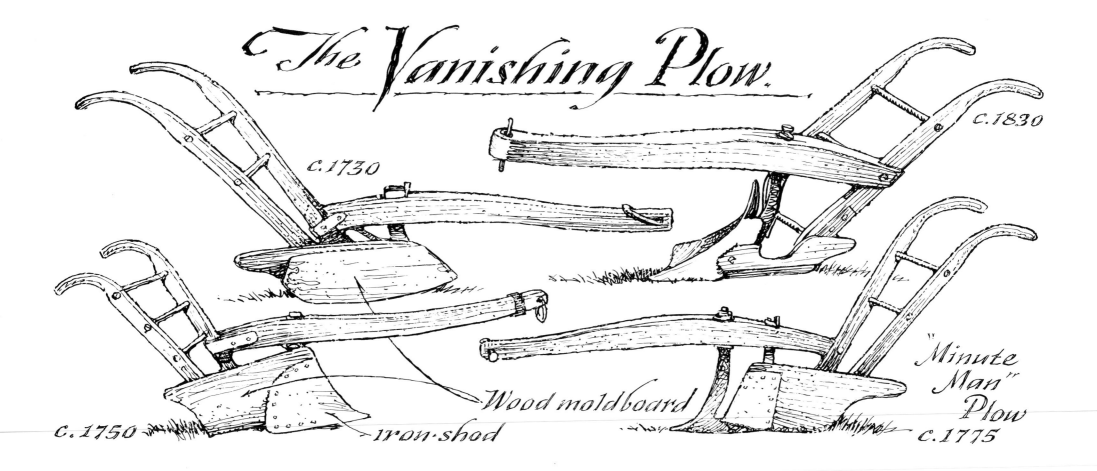

The Vanishing Plow

c.1730

c.1750

iron-shod

Wood moldboard

c.1830

"Minute Man" Plow

c.1775

I AM MORE THAN LIKELY THE ONLY ONE IN THE WORLD with a horse-drawn plow on his living-room table. This is an age when junk sculpture welded from discarded truck parts is accepted as fashionable art, but a plain old country plow is something else again. Yet it is, I do believe, much more a work of art. My Connecticut neighbor Alexander Calder and his followers have had a delicious sense of humor about, as well as a novel approach to, stabile and mobile sculpture; but whether the result be welded from a discarded object or from sheet steel, I still see that discarded object or a sheet steel whatsis instead of any decorative and meaningful art.

It was in the little red barn of my first farm that I found my living-room plow, and for a few years I used it as outdoor sculpture. It was a delight to the eye there, but after a few decades. I finally became aware of its real greatness, so I cleaned it off and moved it indoors. It is now a piece of history, a symphony of early American design, a triumph of mechanical art, and I know I will never see a more graceful, truer work of art.

An old Shaker saying has it that "God invented the circle, religion invented the triangle, and man invented the square." Certainly these three shapes have been richly represented in art lore throughout the ages, but variations of the three shapes produced the plow, which became established as a symbol of civ-

When I first moved to my new Weather Hill Studio, this surrey-plow was in that part of the barn which is now a kitchen. "Move it outside," I told the builder, "and we'll find a place for it later." It has sat there through a few winters now, and I doubt if its wheels will turn now. But rust has turned it to a good red, and it has become a part of the scenery outside my studio window. I suppose it will stay there as long as I live.

Over the hill and a mile or so away lives a famous "modern" sculptor whose landscape is scattered with an intrusion of valuable pieces of welded "art." But my weathered surrey-plow is accepted by its surroundings, a natural ornament to the landscape. A piece of sculpture that no single craftsman could design, it is the result of a thousand "farmer-artists."

Down in the green at New Milford stands a World War I army tank: children climb upon it and the town fathers say it is a fine monument to a fine purpose. Now and then a child climbs up on my surrey-plow monument and drives an imaginary team of oxen ahead of it.

ilization. Its classic curves have evolved over several centuries, each few years its shape changing slightly and enhancing certain subtleties of design; the final result is a harmony of lines that even a master portrait painter would have difficulty portraying. I know, because I've sketched and painted plows, always finding that the slightest deviation from their true lines is jarring and also immediately noticeable. If I were a teacher of art, I might choose the plow as a most exacting subject for students.

Horses have vanished from the farm scene and with them went the horse-drawn plow: within another twenty-five years the plow will have become a rare antique. I have already been offered a few hundred dollars for mine, although the farmer's ancient daybook had it listed as having cost only two dollars and twenty-five cents. I suppose an all-wood plow might now have a value of a thousand dollars or more. It seems strange that such an item, an em-

blem of civilized man, could have vanished within my lifetime.

I remember exhibiting early farm implements and woodworking tools as objects of art at the New Britain Museum of American Art. As a reply to "assemblages," "constructions," and other modern three-dimensional presentations, I simply mounted authentic implements on boards and called them "placements." The president of The Stanley Works attended the opening and asked me if I had considered giving my collection to the public. "I'll do that," I replied, "if you will donate a building for it." A year later, the Sloane-Stanley Museum in Kent, Connecticut, was a reality.

I do believe that implements of traditional design will become more and more recognized as art, and that hand tools, which are really extensions of the human hand, will return to the dignity and respect they deserve and once were given.

Found in my barn, the old horse-drawn plow in this painting is the one that ended as sculpture on my living room table. Before I cleaned it and prepared it for its place of honor, I decided to set it up before the old barn wing and record what had been its home for the last century.

It is interesting how even plaster and stone will often fall away while wood, if properly exposed to the weather, only hardens. The boards from this barn, shrunk from age so that sunlight sifted through the spaces between, brought smoke from my power-saw's blades, so hardened was their inner wood. I suppose the wooden beam on my plow is harder now than it was when it was new, while only its metal shows signs of deterioration.

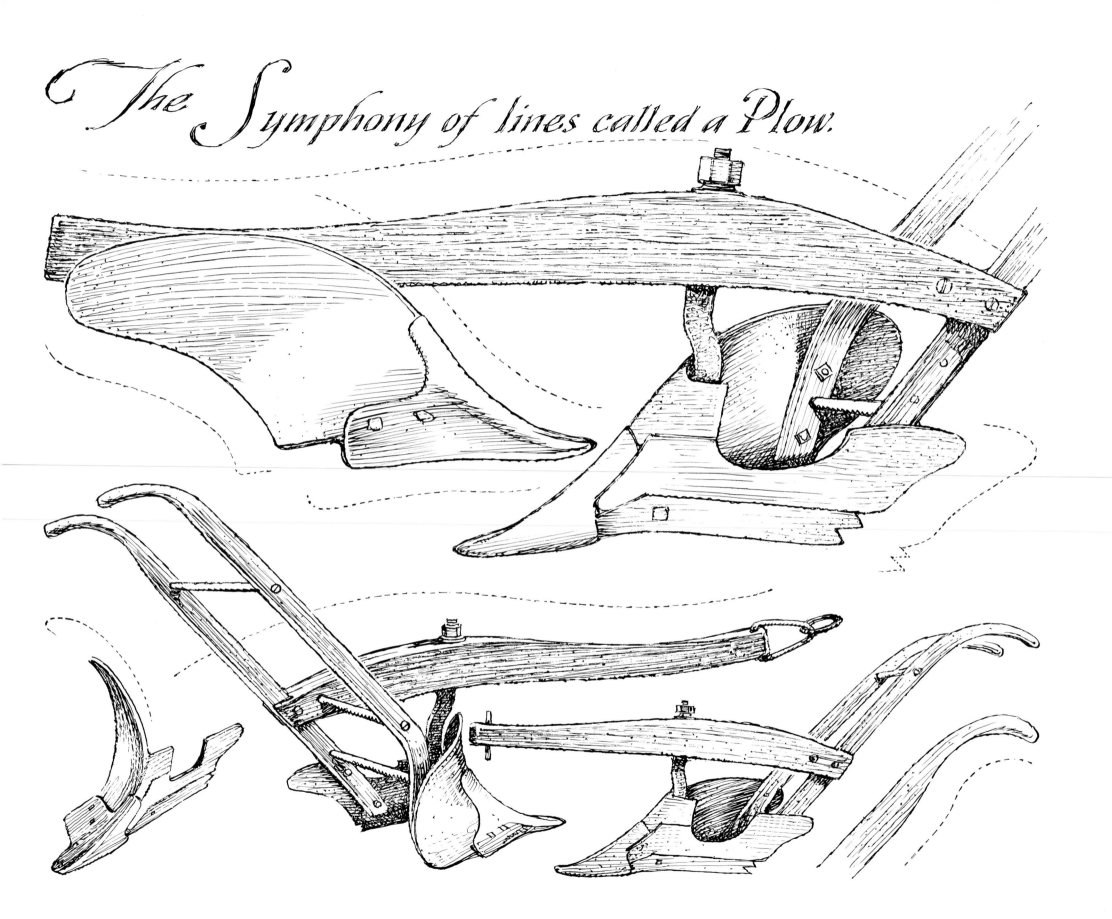

The Symphony of lines called a Plow.

Summer Place...

I REMEMBER WHEN ELECTRICITY WAS BROUGHT ACROSS the lake to the island where I spent summers as a small boy. The darkness, which could be dispelled only by a battery flashlight or the uncertain light of a kerosene lantern, had been part of the wonder and romance of all my vacation nights. But when the flick of a switch exploded night into day, the walk down to the lake lost all its charm, and the nighttime mystery of the shore and the cavernous boathouse was no more. That modern convenience ended part of a wondrous world that I would never experience again.

Father had built an icehouse near the Lake. I remember that his workmen hit rock and had to blast most of the house from solid granite, but when it was finished, he was very proud. Opening the trapdoor, climbing down into the wet hay, and hoisting fifty-pound cakes of lake ice was man's work, but it was part of vacation fun for a young boy. When electricity came and the old kitchen porch icebox was turned into a storage bin, the icehouse was abandoned. Electricity had ended not only my chore of getting ice each week, but also the work of gathering and polishing all the lamp globes. My Saturdays had lost something. "Some day," said my father, "I'll find some use for the icehouse." But he never did.

I can remember crushing lake ice to pack around an ice-cream freezer . . . feeding the collar of ice with rock salt . . . turning the crank until the work began to be difficult. Then, opening the canister, seeing the rich yellowish whip of crunchy homemade ice cream, and licking the wooden paddles dry! I fear those things are all joys of the past for I've already seen hand-turned ice-cream freezers in antique stores; and the only ice cream we know is a foamy blown-up whip that you suck in rather than sink your teeth into.

After electricity dealt its death blow to father's icehouse, I decided I could earn some money selling the leftover lake ice that was still in the icehouse. That was the year when Red Grange prepared for his football season by working as a summertime iceman, so my decision was somewhat fashionable. The project ended soon after I put a huge piece of not very clear ice in a neighbor's icebox: when it melted he learned how, in ice-cutting season, horses were used to help with the harvesting of the ice. What was left in his icebox was a great load of manure that had been frozen inside the ice!

The summer place today has become a different establishment with a cellar, central heat, electric lights, and all the accoutrements of a year-round house, but a real summer place one time meant a complete vacation from all mechanical conveniences; it was a retreat to nature, a period of rest and meditation, a vacating from the city world.

Summer houses had names. You would paint the name on a wooden plaque and hang it over the porch or on the boathouse. My family's place was called "Cedarcrest," and the place next door was "Pinewood." Across the lake were "Sans Souci," "Island View," "Bon Air," and "The Cove House." Smaller places seemed to favor Indian names like "Camp Hiawatha" and "The Teepee."

No summer place was complete without a number of brightly colored hammocks; not skimpy ones like those made today but big soft-pillowed jobs with twelve-inch fringe. When Columbus arrived to find the Indians sleeping in "hanging beds made of bark from the hamack tree," he reported something truly American; it seems a shame the hammock has deteriorated rather than having enjoyed improvement.

There were also rolled split-bamboo screens that were lowered to shade the porch, and striped canvas awnings that from the inside made each window a shadowbox for long-remembered summer scenes. At night you opened windows and stretched accordion-like framed, wooden screens across the openings. Sitting on the porch in the dark, with scented punk sticks to challenge the lightning bugs, families actually said things to one another as rockers squeaked an accompaniment.

"The day should be divided into three parts," my father used to tell me. "Eight hours for work, eight hours for sleep, and eight hours for play. And the year should be divided into three parts too, with three full months for vacation." I remember him opening our summer place every year on Memorial Day. He always left for the city on Labor Day, but for the rest

of us the actual closing and boarding up against the winter extended another few weeks into the height of the crimson foliage of Indian Summer.

Closing a summer house in autumn was less of a chore than it was a ceremony. I recall that we went about it with very little talk, like relatives attending a family funeral. Rockers on the porch were tipped and leaned against the wall. For nine months the solid wooden shutters would close in the tastes of a spent summer and the warm memories of vacation against a stark, abandoned countryside. The front storm door would be shut and locked with a hook from the inside, and after you locked the dark house with a key in the back kitchen door, the immense inner sadness of a closed vacation place took over.

Opening the summer house was also a profound experience. The stale air of each room and the dank smells of empty bureau drawers gave way to air from open windows and doors that let in the good odors of spring. Only in the country did breakfasts seem to smell the way breakfasts should; the pungency of coffee and the smoke from wet, raked-up leaves burning outside made an unforgettable ceremonial incense. In fact everything seemed at that time to acquire an abundance of odor. Everything, that is, except the water, which, fortunately, had not the

Beach house...

143

I suppose this painting might serve to answer the never-ending question endured by painters: "How long did it take to paint?" Seeking to recapture the sort of American summer place I knew as a child, I did over two dozen examples in a year, all of which I destroyed. After another year of searching, I found what I wanted and did this painting in something like three hours. I would say it took me about two years and three hours to produce a satisfactory painting.

I found the subject when I remembered the summer "bungalows" of my youth. As an iceman (or iceboy) during one summer, I delivered to hundreds of vacationers in these frame shorefront houses. During late autumn when the places were closed, the weather made the countryside so much more impressive, and the aura of carefree vacation turned to one of profound melancholy.

As I stopped at the porch of this shuttered house, I asked myself aloud if this was the subject I'd been looking for. And as if for no reason whatsoever, a rotted tree a few hundred feet away shuddered and collapsed with a roar that broke the silence of Indian Summer. It was frightening, and I considered my question well answered.

smell of piped city water. But if odorless, it was deliciously cold—and, as you drank it from the tin dipper, like no other water.

Here and there you will find such a decaying summer place where iron water pumps and iceboxes and outhouses and kerosene lamps were accessories of a vacation household; when gone, such places will never return. And neither will the strange awareness of and precious closeness to nature that created the richness of yesterday's summer places.

Spring Houses

IF OUR PRESENT DAY WATER SUPPLY AND REFRIGERA-tors were frequently infested with snakes, insects, and the bodies of dead animals, we might realize why Great-Great-Grandfather was well equipped with iron hooks to grope into his well and clear it out every few days. Without an electric flashlight there was no way to see into the darkness below (kerosene lamps couldn't shine downward) so this chore was as often a precaution as a necessity. Many farmers lowered fruit, butter, and meats into the well to keep them cool, so there were also lost pails and some-times spilled food to retrieve. The best-designed

farmhouse had a springhouse, which was sort of an aboveground well: the springhouse was yesterday's standard refrigerator.

Springhouses, usually made of stone and mortar, have usually outlasted other farm buildings; except for a cleaning out, many springhouses even two cen-turies old would now be in usable condition. But man has so changed the water level within the last few decades that some of the springs have vanished. My friend General Wolf of Blue Bell, Pennsylvania, uses the ancient springhouse of his home as a cider and wine cellar, and I suppose the temperatures in

The spring house was often the first building erected on a farm and from its nails and manner of construction, the researcher can usually find a clue to the age of a farmstead.

Attached to a stone barn, this typical spring house is one I happened upon in Pennsylvania. Like many others, it has a separate room above the spring room, used for storing whatever needs cooling but with less dampness. A virtual duplicate of this building stands a few yards from the old Chad homestead in Chadd's Ford; its upper room was converted into a schoolroom at one time and a fireplace was added.

The New England spring house was more often a low shed or only a roof resting on stones located on a hill higher than the house; by gravity feed the spring supplied the homestead kitchen with constantly running water.

near Marshallton.

at Chester Springs.

House entrance to Springhouse.

it are the same throughout this year as they were in 1760. The book of plans the original builder used is still in my library.

"The main points in making a springhouse" [it reads] "are coolness of water, purity of air, perfect drainage, and a steady temperature throughout the year.

"The first is secured by locating the house near the spring, which must be dug out, cleaned, and arched over with proper stonework. A spout carries the water to the house, into a trough at hip level for holding crocks of food and bottles of liquids. Furniture of hemlock boards may accommodate cream jars and butter bowls; otherwise no wood is used.

151

This springhouse near an old barn outside of Lumberville, Pennsylvania, was one that sheltered me from a lightning storm during a sketching tour. The desolate barn, too, was empty, but my knowledge that barns often attract lightning because of the static electricity accumulated in old hay led me to the protection of the springhouse and its long, slanted roof.

Now, some two dozen years later, I suppose the barn has collapsed (it had already started then), but I'd wager the spring-house is as good as it was in the 1700's.

Milk is placed in the coldest part of the flowing pool within the trough, with jars and stone pots nearer the outlet. Light is no disadvantage to the springhouse and a plastering of lime brings added illumination."

The use of stone rather than wood is scientifically interesting for it proves how the old-timers were aware that stone maintains low temperatures better than wood. In Pennsylvania even the furniture of springhouses was made of stone. One stone table in a Bucks County springhouse was of three-inch slate and measured three by six feet. I am sure an interesting book might be done about ancient springhouses; in fact, it is strange that so important a building of yesterday has been neglected. I went to visit the Andrew Wyeths one time and never did reach their house because there were so many extraordinary examples of early springhouses in and around Chadds Ford that I spent the whole day collecting them in my sketchbook. I realized then how Wyeth could find such rich and continuing sources of inspiration from so confined an area. And how after almost half a century of painting, his work rises above mere nostalgia and champions nature itself.

Spring House, Chester County Pa.

This is the Bee Brook milk house about six miles from my place. It was made from brick manufactured right on the farm, and the roof was of slate quarried on the same property.

Springhouses were used for many purposes: this one is now just a storage building, but I often wondered in what other ways it had been used. Friends recently dropped by my studio, and neighbor Marge Tanner immediately spotted this painting. "My old milk house!" she exclaimed. "I used to race around inside that little milk house when I was four years old! The water was in a pool in the very center and we kept two tame trout in it. We used to put cans of milk right in the water, to keep them cold. The raised shelf inside that I used to run around was designed for storing butter and eggs." She ran her hand around her sturdy waist. "I sure couldn't run around in it now, though. Wonder if I could even get inside!"

Harvest then and Now.

THOSE NEATLY TIED SQUARISH PACKAGES OF HAY THAT the baler drops off here and there across our few remaining hayfields wrap up a lot of beautiful memories of early American life into Picasso-like symbols of mechanized farming. Now there is no group of farmers—only one loud tractor. No laughter or singing, no switchel of molasses, water, ginger, and vinegar to drink, no horses and haywagons; even scythes and pitchforks are gone. The only thing unchanged is the odor of cut grass and the strange and faraway inherited sense of autumn and harvest time.

No boy should be deprived of the experience of harvesting. Beside the value of feeling the fruition of nature all about you, there is the satisfaction of beholding the results of your own efforts. I suppose the frustration of youth nowadays comes from being deprived of worthwhile things to do and the satisfaction derived from having accomplished something.

I remember many harvests, when haying was the first act in the drama of autumn. Before it was invaded, the meadow was a constantly changing carpet of grasses and blossoms; when it was cut, there was something sad and final about the scene. The grass shuddered apprehensively a little ahead of the mowing machine; then it was hit and cut by blades moving too fast to be seen. The second act began when the hay tedder kicked up the fallen grass and showered the air with clouds of pollen and meadow perfume. Then, after a proper intermission of weather, the horse-drawn rake gathered the cured hay into windrows. And the last act was always the most stirring, when men pitched the windrows into cocks and finally lifted the haycocks into a wagon, ready for storing.

My dog used to follow me to each windrow of hay, watching me as I lifted them away and into the wagon, for nearly each one held a family or two of

This scene extended beyond my first studio at Warren, Connecticut. The opposite ridge, in Milton, shoulders a back road to Litchfield. When I first moved there, the popular belief was that you could earn enough to pay the land taxes by selling the rights to your hay. But it turned out that just hiring a farmer to keep the fields cut (along with free hay to him) cost nearly as much as the taxes.

It was worth it, however, to smell the perfume of cut grass, watch it being raked and waggoned and hauled away. Now the work is done by machines and the process of harvest is less exciting. But there will always be something in man that reacts to the scene of harvest as being meaningful, close to the earth, and, if you are a religious person, close to God.

meadow mice. He never did catch a mouse, as I recall, but the pleasure of finding them and chasing them was a wild game he looked forward to at each harvest time.

Next to the plow, the early American hand sickle impresses me as being the most aesthetically designed implement to have evolved from a thousand subtle variations throughout the centuries. One might think a simple curve easy to recall and reproduce; yet it seems nearly impossible, and the slightest change becomes noticeable at once. Almost in desperation, instead of copying a sickle, I had to trace it. I consider it remarkable that this exquisite curve has always been the same, although the sickle was reproduced in various parts of America and made by many different men. The reaping crook or

hay hook also had an exquisite curve. The sickle and hook were used together—the hook pulled a swatch of grass toward you and the sickle cut it. I have found several hay hooks and discovered the same delicate curve in each one.

The same oddity occurs with all harvesting implements. I have collected "bull rakes," handmade during the middle 1700s and early 1800s; those from the West, the South, the Atlantic coast, and New England are alike almost to the inch, and all appear to have been made by the same person. For a long time it was tradition that influenced the design of tools. And harvest time was so moving that it seemed to be the most festive time of the earliest American years, and so Thanksgiving, not Christmas, was the first American holiday.

The Sickle... and the Reaping Crook.

Many describe Kansas as "where you can look farther without seeing anything," but I remember it as the place where a person can see the most sky. The sky in Kansas has a peculiar affinity to the land, and the land resembles the sea in many ways—in its immensity and in the waves that occur in the wheatfields when the wind blows. Like lighthouses, those sentinels of scattered farms—the windmills— are dwarfed by the vastness of the sky. I remember "piloting" a tractor combine and using a distant windmill as a guide to keep my machine on a straight path, almost as one might head a ship for a certain target. And I am still trying to forget the poor job I did by zigzagging toward the horizon.

But remember Kansas and you will automatically remember the sky.

I REMEMBER A MOST UNUSUAL BATH. HIKING ACROSS the desert country in midsummer was a foolish whim, but at seventeen I didn't think so. In the Southwest, where towns are marked by water towers and farms are spotted by windmills, I had walked for a night and day without water when, over the horizon, I saw what appeared to be a distant windmill. When I reached the spot, I found only an abandoned mine, but there was an ancient windmill still pumping a trickle of water into an old iron bathtub that, I guess, had served to make a reservoir for

167

horses. By the time the water reached the tub (coming through a long metal pipe from a hill to the horse corral), it was piping hot. I wiped the sand and scum from the ancient tub, and with the aid of soap that I carried in my sign-painter's knapsack I had a most extraordinary bath on the outskirts of the Mojave Desert.

Remembering windmills and extolling their virtues seemed a bit of antiquarian whimsy at first and I winced at my own fascination of such bygone Americana. But Stewart L. Udall, the former Secretary of the Interior whose complete heart and mind were in his work, gave me encouragement. "Ecologically speaking," he said, "the windmill is one of the earth's few perfect devices. It harnesses a completely free source of power to pump water under conditions that respect the laws and limits of nature. In Arizona, western Texas and other arid places of the Southwest, electric pumps deplete groundwater stored up over the centuries by geological processes. The costs of such exploitation are already evident in the fast-growing thirst for 'replacement' water from Canada and Alaska. But ranchers who still use windmills to tap near-surface water for their livestock (taking only as much as is replaced each year) face no such crisis: they are working with nature."

The windmill accepts a God-given natural power, uses up no natural resource and expels no pollution into the atmosphere. Like the waterwheel and the sailboat it has a Zero Environmental Impact (ZEI) and more than being a creaky sentiment of a bygone age, it is a peculiar symbol of sanity for a world hopelessly hooked on machines with ever increasing hunger for fuel and capacity to pollute.

Perhaps the most promising industry of the American Midwest after the Civil War was the manufacture of windmills. About five hundred patented models were being made, and Batavia, Illinois, with three major factories was once known as "Windmill City." Before that, homemade full-sized Dutch windmills were being erected in all the prairie states. Kansas actually had windmills to match those in Holland; the biggest Dutch windmill in the world was in San Francisco, with a spread of 114 feet. Two of these sail-type windmills pumped 70,000 gallons of water an hour for the Golden Gate Park.

There are still remote places in America, beyond the reach of electricity, where wind pumps water from the ground. And it was only a century ago that there were about a quarter of a million wind-powered mills pumping water, sawing wood, grinding corn, churning butter, turning grindstones, shelling corn, chopping oats and doing other farm chores. In 1900 the Sears Roebuck catalogue listed three grades of windmills, from an eight-foot span at nineteen dollars to an eighteen-foot span at one hundred and ninety. Water was not always available for turning mill wheels, and during winter most water-powered mill wheels were frozen to a standstill until the spring thaw. So the American windmill was more popular than most people realize. I have found early American lore full of references to windmills. The New York ferries, for example, were regulated to run only when the surrounding windmills were operating. Service was shut down "when the windmills on the battery of Manhattan hath taken down or lowered their sails because of consequence of storm or otherwise." The windmill was one of the first items to frighten the Indians, I learned when I unearthed an account of how they stayed at a safe distance from the "great arms that turned with the wind and chewed cornmeal and flour."

the Cape Cod coastline..

Nantucket

Chatham

Eastham

..and the

Kansas prairies!

Only a
Sod home but
a great windmill

The Atlantic coast, as early as 1640, was dotted with windmills, and sailors took their sightings by known mill towers, which were even indicated on marine maps. On the flatlands of New Jersey and Long Island, where streams were not available for water power, all mills ran by wind; Cape Cod was clustered with them. Thousands of small (some even portable) mills pumped seawater into the flats, where it was converted into salt. I painted one, the Old East Mill, at Orleans, Massachusetts, near Cape Cod. It was like a nostalgic dream to paint it again so many years later at Sandwich, Massachusetts, where it had been moved and restored by my friend Josiah Lilly, III. And there today the Old East Mill is at work again!

169

The Mills of America

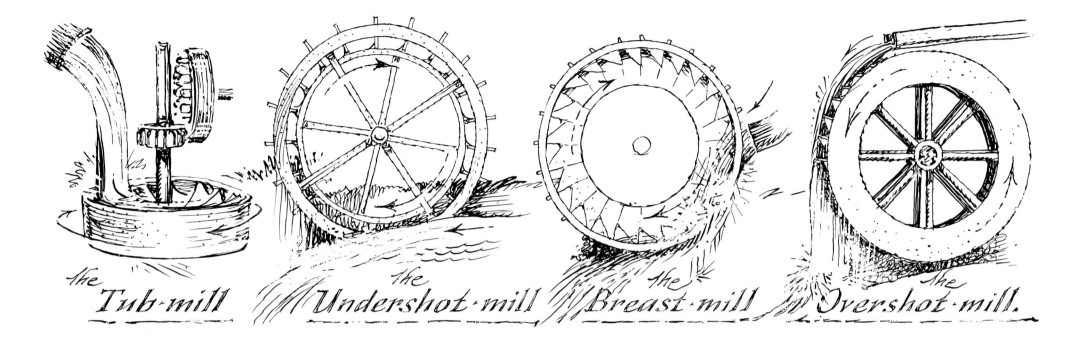

the **Tub-mill**   the **Undershot-mill**   the **Breast-mill**   the **Overshot-mill.**

A SHORT DISTANCE FROM MY LAND IN CONNECTICUT is a hilltop area known as Dudleytown. Once it was a busy village; now the place is famous as a ghost town. Actually the overgrown forest has left no evidence whatsoever of habitation, but eerie trail names such as "Dark Entry Road" and "Owlsboro Lane" help keep alive a false legend of the village and its ancient curse. Strange happenings and mysterious deaths are supposed to have occurred there. One lady was hit by a lightning bolt, and a man died "mysteriously at the age of ninety-eight," but I am sure it was as normal a community as any of those of the early 1700s. I've camped out there, but my hopes of seeing the spirit of old Abiel Dudley, a spirit that is supposed to appear during the full moon, were never realized.

In those days naming a village after anything but a town in England or a name from the Bible was supposed to result in a curse. Naming it after John Dudley, who had lost his head by royal decree, was courting special disaster. Yet the true reason for Dudleytown's becoming a ghost village involves the much more interesting story of American watermills.

In the beginning, it seems, pioneers settled only on high ground; it offered protection from marauding Indians and from beasts. Furthermore, the low land was dark, full of mire and swamp; only high ground was considered healthful. Dudleytown was, therefore, founded atop a cleared hill in the Berkshires.

After a few decades of farming out the high land, men began to consider the possibilities of turning to manufacturing. Connecticut scientists had worked out a way of getting tremendous power from overshot waterwheels. These had twice the efficiency of European undershot and breast wheels, and so wa-

The overhanging roof of this mill afforded protection for a farmer's wagon while his corn was being ground. Overhanging roofs seem to be vanished Americana; even gasoline stations subject their attendants (and the gasoline tanks, too) to rain and the elements, and I wonder why.

This mill has now burned, its wheel hangs at a drunken angle over the tumbling brook, and one of the millstones found there has become the outside step at the entrance of my studio. I always feel guilty about using an old millstone, recalling Deuteronomy (xxiv: 6):

No man shall take the nether or the upper millstone to pledge; for he taketh a man's life to pledge.

A broken and decaying mill seems to have a poignant message. As the stream still moves past the useless wheel, I recall the saying: "The mill will never grind with water that is past."

termills began to appear all along the rivers and streams. Soon other buildings were erected near the mills, and the mill complex was established. Every state had a Milton, a Milbrook, a Milford, a Milwood, and other mill hamlets that grew rapidly into villages. Then the pioneers abandoned their hilltop farms by the hundreds. Dudleytown moved into the valley, where the mills were.

Over the past two centuries mill villages have grown into mill towns and mill cities. Countless numbers of major factories suffer almost yearly flooding because of the New England stubbornness to "stay put," even though electricity has come and waterwheels are long gone. Only within the last few decades have we begun to move back to high land; a cycle is finally perhaps being completed. And I suspect that some day Dudleytown will be reborn.

I once thought of doing a book about the early American watermills. But a trip through the southern watermill country netted me only a sketchbook full of quaintness, obsolescence, and decaying wooden machinery. Whatever water could do, gasoline or electricity seemed to do better. The waterwheel, my publishers and I decided, was a dead subject.

I did learn, however, that before the Pilgrims arrived, several watermills in Maine and Newfoundland were grinding out corn for export. This rather explodes the schoolboy legend of the Pilgrims being first to set foot on the northeast coast. The actual map they used for reaching their destination listed not only "Plymouth" in its true location but also other nearby settlements such as Dartmouth, Ipswich, Norwich, Southampton, Oxford, Boston, and Hull. One year before the Pilgrims landed at Plymouth Rock, Ferdinando Gorges, who had obtained a grant

from the English crown to develop land near what is now South Berwick, Maine), gave proof of his agreement to build a mill there by sending back his first shipment of ground cornmeal. Three years before the Pilgrim's landing, Pocahontas had died in London!

After pollution finally prohibits the use of heat motors, I predict, man will return in desperation to water power. Even now about a third of all the electricity we use is manufactured by water power; a few years back nearly all industry depended upon it. I still find watermills and waterpower exciting lore of American history. And I still remember the last remaining watermills.

The old mill house and the leisurely sloshing of the waterwheel give the impression of rustic lassitude. But from within things are different. I recall when a millwright in the Tennessee mountains let me start his machinery; the weight of the water suddenly seemed to fill the building with its immensity. The strain of power was felt in every timber and the whole building swayed as the unseen wheel began to turn. Twelve-by-sixteen oak beams shuddered, ton-heavy wooden gears squealed, and millstones ground so loudly that you had to shout to make your voice heard.

Starting machinery, no matter how powerful it may be, is without romance or excitement if it involves only the pressing of a button or the turning of a switch. You don't even know exactly where the power comes from. But when you loose a thousand tons of water over a massive waterwheel, there is a special and overwhelming awareness of power that makes you feel a part of the machine and the machine a part of you. I can understand why the miller lived his profession and died with it.

This is probably how the old East Mill looked when it first caught the breezes of Cape Cod in 1800. Reverend Jonathan Bascom of the Congregational Meeting House in Orleans donated timbers from his church for the building of this mill, which later ground corn for the Union Army during the Civil War. The last grist was swept from its stones in 1893, and its rotting sails were put away.

Like many early windmills, it has been moved from one place to another and treated as a rare curiosity in this day of engine power. Only a few like it remain. Perhaps they might serve as a symbol of a mechanical power that offers no pollution. We need more of that sort of power.

Choo Choo!

AT A CUB SCOUT MEETING ONE AFTERNOON, I DID A verbal imitation of a train's wailing whistle, and the chugging of the locomotive pulling uphill and finally coming to a stop with much puffing and hissing of steam. I found my youthful audience totally unimpressed and wondered why. Then I realized that none of them had ever seen or heard a steam locomotive; to them it was just a lot of strange noises. It made me feel really old—yet it was only fifteen years

ago when I could step aboard the dining car of a train at the Cornwall Bridge station in Connecticut, and by the time my newspaper had been read and my coffee finished, I was in New York City, fresh for a day's work. Today that railroad station is closed, abandoned and going to rot. Other stations north and south of it have been sold or are rented as shops: the Cornwall Bridge station is too far gone now to have any value except as firewood.

Once a week a lone freight train uses the tracks some six miles south, still blasting the night air with an approach signal as it grinds past the boarded-up Cornwall Bridge passenger station. The high-pitched hoot of the Diesel horn startles me as I lie in bed, and in the darkness I remember and miss the old-time, steam-train whistle. Unlike the rude shrillness of a Diesel horn, the sound of a steam-train whistle was comforting; it seemed to have a soul and it spoke many greetings.

I recall being on the prairies, after I'd left home as a young man, and how the whistle of a lighted train as it rushed through the black night brought many images to my mind. One of the clearest of these was of my father consulting his watch when he heard the ten-o'clock train. "She's right on time," he'd say, "and it's time for bed." The whistle was like a human voice, and it could be informative, friendly or sad, urging or soothing, but never angry. To farm lads it spoke of high adventure, to parents of visits from children who had gone to seek that adventure, and to traveling salesmen of their families back home.

Few things American are disappearing as fast as are the railroads. The trusts and transportation combines controlling roadway construction, oil refining, and automotive manufacture must be enormously powerful to be able to defy the national need for

179

The old time American railroad station with its overhanging roof and ornamental braces, was a rare contribution to American architecture, worthy of recording. Yet only antique value seems to bring it any attention now.

The shadow in the foreground of this painting is from a new concrete arch spanning the Housatonic. It replaced a nearby covered-bridge site, leaving the abandoned railroad station overpassed and disintegrating into the landscape. Two churches, a store and a post office once joined to make it a busy station. Now, all the stations along the Housatonic are a line of architectural ghosts connected by historic rails.

It has been my hope to buy the Cornwall Bridge station and railroad it southward to the site of my museum of early American tools as a permanent exhibit. Certainly the railroad has been a major tool in the creating of our country, with a past too exciting to be easily forgotten.

railroads and cause such disgraceful decay. I suppose when highways finally crowd out enough human living space, and when automobile gases so saturate the atmosphere that trucking is outlawed, we shall try to buy back the lands lost by bankrupt railroad lines and start anew!

From John Stevens' locomotive of 1824 to the 120 mph train of 1901, America was built and served well by its railroads, but since then the picture changed. Today Japan and France have the fastest and the best rail service, while America's commuters can only complain—in vain.

The American railroad has been sick and deteriorating slowly, but 1971 marked the end, after the long illness, in many places, as century old passenger stations become vanishing Americana. In May of 1971, the last train pulled away from Miles City, Montana, its bell seeming to toll rather than ring for the last time. Other towns along the line, like Billings and Glendive and Forsyth, joined the funeral procession. And a thousand names like Barnesville, Georgia, and Harpers Ferry, West Virginia, that played major parts in history stand in line for the same indignity.

I will never forget the one year in which I spent more than twelve hundred hours on commuter trains. But I also recall clean cars, comfortable seats, windows that opened and closed and were clear enough to see through. Thomas was the name of the conductor on the train I nearly always rode, and he considered his passengers as members of his family. He would do errands for you in the city if you hadn't the time to go in; on more than one occasion he delivered paintings and manuscripts for me during his lunch hour. When the train was discontinued, his "family" gave him a gold watch and five hundred dollars.

In those days trains were parlors, reading rooms, offices on wheels; now they are more like cattle cars. It seems strange (almost grotesque) that modern man can fly around the world at tremendous speed and in relative comfort, with drinks and music and movies and personal service; yet he cannot ride to or from work with either speed or comfort.

Just think of the almost countless billions that have been spent in sending a few men to a dead moon, while transportation to and from daily work in a living world is dying! We are so engrossed with engineering and mechanization that we seem to have lost sight of our own living species. There is an insidious logic that men must adapt to machines instead of machines to men; that production, speed, novelty and progress at any price must come first, and people second.

I refuse to adapt myself to dirt and discomfort, so I have ceased commuting, but I often go down to the Cornwall Bridge railroad station and think about the time when machinery adapted itself to people and the result was good.

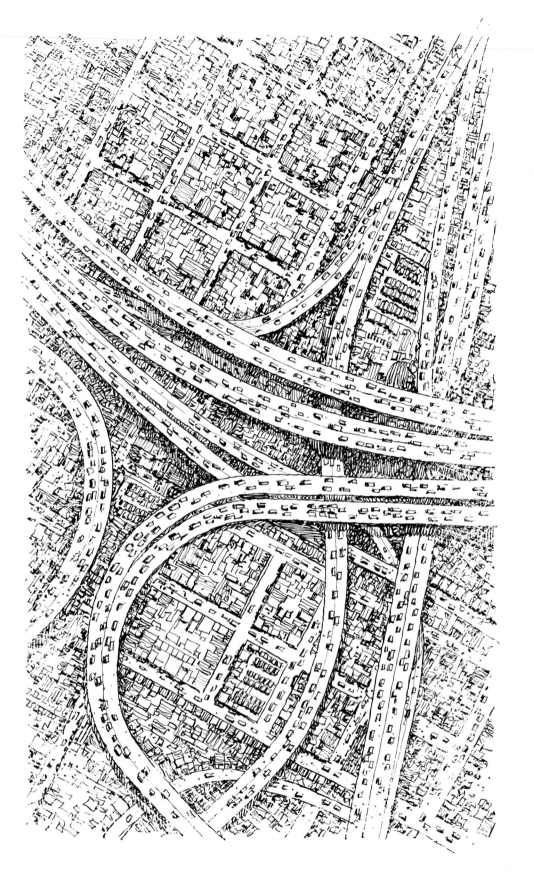

NOW MY BOOK IS DONE, AND AS I GLANCE BACK through the manuscript, I realize its argument is not with America but with the whole world. After having survived about a hundred million years by adapting to our original habitat—the earth with its rivers and mountains and seas and forests—civilization is suddenly confronted with the possibility of running out of living space.

The greatest changes in humanity occurred within my lifetime, and I am grateful for having so many good things to remember—things that youth today and tomorrow will never see or feel. It is regrettable that all the things my parents lived for, as well as the objects and the joys of work and simple living, as I have described them in the foregoing pages, may be regarded only as folklore or merely nostalgic yearning on my part for what today's world considers to be obsolescence.

"Sloane writes about America with fondness and honesty," said a *New York Times* critic, "and he will be popular as long as he is never bitter."

I suppose that by having written and illustrated this book, I risk becoming unpopular. But it is really not bitterness I feel: it is anger and sadness. Albert Schweitzer, an honest and patient man without rancor, diagnosed civilization in this way: "Man has lost the capacity to foresee and to forestall. Man will end by destroying the earth."

Those are harsh words from a patient man, and although I agree with Schweitzer, I still have a phoenix hope: that, while the America of early time is now dead, there will be a great rebirth of our country, one that will incorporate the many things of our past that are better than what we have at present. Thus, I hope my remembrance of America may have a purpose for the future.